T0169096

**Footprint** Handbook

# Salvador &
# Bahia

ALEX & GARDÊNIA ROBINSON

# This is
## Salvador &
## Bahia

White-sand beaches backed by coconut palms, steep winding streets lined with pastel-coloured houses, ornate baroque churches, Afro-Brazilian ceremonies, the rhythm of the *berimbau* and the swirling dance of capoeira …

Bahia conjures up as many exotic images, sounds and smells as Rio de Janeiro and has an equally strong claim to be the heart of Brazil. The state capital, Salvador, was the country's first city for far longer than any other, and remains one of the country's cultural centres.

Brazil's most famous novelist, Jorge Amado, was a Bahian, as were many of its greatest musicians; it was Bahia that gave the world samba, capoeira, Carnaval and *candomblé*. The state has some of the best cuisine in the country, along with many of its best beaches. Bahia's beautiful coast stretches far to the north and south of Salvador and is dotted with resorts along its length: laid-back little places like Itacaré, Morro de São Paulo and Trancoso, and larger more hedonistic party towns like Porto Seguro and Arraial d'Ajuda.

Inland, in the wild semi-desert of the Sertão, is one of Brazil's premier hiking destinations, the Chapada Diamantina, whose towering escarpments are cut by clear-water rivers and dotted with plunging waterfalls.

*Alex Robinson*

*Gardenia Robinson*

# Best of
## Salvador &
## Bahia

### ❶ Salvador

Brazil's first capital offers an impressive old colonial centre, the Pelourinho. Spend a morning wandering its cobbled streets, dotted with glittering golden baroque churches. Don't miss its lively carnival, one of Brazil's best. Page 26.

### ❷ Salvador's Afro-Brazilian culture

Attend a *candomblé* religious ceremony, lunch on *moqueca de camarão*, the quintessential Bahian dish, in the Axego restaurant, listen to the Olodum band pound out *afoxé* rhythms, learn capoeira and visit the villages of the Recôncavo, where samba was born. Pages 33, 46, 48 and 60.

**3**

### 3 Morro de São Paulo

Dance *forró*, dine on spicy Bahian food and wander the long, dreamy beaches that line this tiny island, a mere boat ride from Salvador's docks. Take your pick from five beaches, which get increasingly quiet the further from town you go. Page 64.

### 4 Itacaré

Learn to surf on one of the half a dozen, coconut-shaded beaches that surround this fashionable little beach town, with a relaxed fishing village feel in its centre. Hotels backing the beaches range from high-end to hippy. Page 70.

## ❺ Atlantic coastal rainforests

Explore the remnant tropical rainforests along the Bahian coast, including the large swathes in the Estação Veracel Vercruz reserve and Monte Pascoal national park in the south, many of them dotted with indigenous villages. Pages 83 and 88.

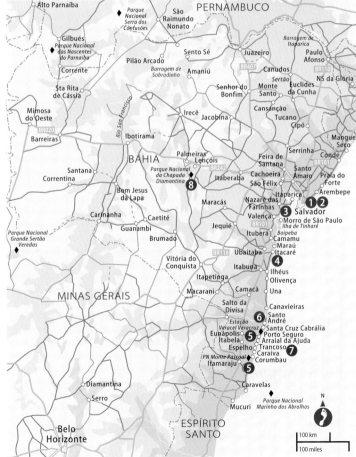

## ⓺ Santo André

Take boat trips to reef-ringed islets and unwind in one of the low-key beachside *pousadas* in this little fishing village surrounded by mangrove forest, north of Porto Seguro. Page 84.

## ⓻ Trancoso and Caraíva

Spend a while in Brazil's capital of barefoot luxury, to wander the vast empty beaches between Trancoso and Caraíva, unwind in a modish boutique hotel and eat alfresco in some of Brazil's best restaurants. Pages 87 and 88.

## ⓼ Parque Nacional da Chapada Diamantina

Hike the dramatic, waterfall-covered mountains and *cerrado* forests in the Bahian interior. For sweeping views over the park, warmed by golden light, climb to the top of the Morro do Pai Inácio in the late afternoon. Pages 104 and 105.

Morro de São Paulo

# Route planner

Covering an area the size of Spain bristling with baroque architecture, fringed with beautiful coconut-shaded beaches, dotted with little fishing villages and broken by rugged table-top mountains with great hiking, Bahia is a destination in its own right. And as things move at a leisurely pace in the state it's a good idea to unwind and take your time over a visit. Consider flying into Salvador and out of Porto Seguro (perhaps with a connection to Rio and beyond) to maximize your time.

## One to two weeks
### Afro-Brazilian culture, waterfalls, beaches

You will be able to take a whistle-stop tour of Salvador, the Chapada Diamantina and one of the northern Bahian beaches, such as Morro de São Paulo, in a week or two. Take a full day to explore Salvador's historical centre, and if you have more than a week spend a day or two learning capoeira, sampling the city's nightlife and taking a day trip to the Recôncavo region to the west, where much of modern Afro-Brazilian culture was born. Then fly or take a bus to the Chapada Diamantina and spend two to three days exploring the park's waterfalls, *cerrado* forests, caves and table-top mountains. If you have time, take a day or even a multi-day trek to get out into the park's wilds and absorb the magnificent scenery.

You will then have to return to Salvador to visit the Bahian coast. Fast catamarans leave from the city docks for the idyllic island of Tinharé where you can relax in the sun for a few days. Morro de São Paulo, the island's main village, sits on a small cape next to a series of magnificent beaches and has a lively nightlife and a broad choice of restaurants and places to stay. Life is so tranquil in Tinharé's other main village that even climbing out of a hammock seems strenuous.

With two weeks you can extend your trip further south to the modish resort of Trancoso – which has perhaps the best beaches in the state – or to the little beach town of Itacaré, where locals take time out from surfing to sell hippy-chic handicrafts on the town's single main street. From here it's straightforward to organize a side trip to the lonely beaches and bays of the Peninsula de Maraú, just to the north.

A three- to four-week trip will allow you to visit Salvador and around, finishing up in southern Bahia. Brazil began here in 1500 when a ship full of Portuguese explorers was blown off course to a sugary beach, where they met Bahia's indigenous Tupi-speaking people.

There are still indigenous villages here today and many of the lonely beaches still feel almost as unspoilt and unknown to Westerners as they must have felt in 1500. Using the beach towns of Arraial d'Ajuda (which is a suburb of Porto Seguro) or Trancoso as a base, take a week or so to explore these beaches by bus or hire car, driving south on the dirt road to tiny Caraíva. While you do so take time to learn some capoeira in Arraial or watch the daily afternoon football match on the Quadrado village green in Trancoso. Browse that town's fashionable little boutiques and restaurants or sample Arraial or Porto Seguro's energetic beach-based nightlife. And visit the old colonial centre of Porto Seguro, and the indigenous Pataxó community at Jaqueira, just to that city's north.

After a few days of activity interspersed with doing not very much at all, take two more days to head further south, with a tour operator like **Mata N'ativa Travel** or **Portomondo** (see page 95). Spend a day exploring the remote stretches of coast between Caraíva and Caravelas, where you can overnight. The following day take a trip to the rocky, reef-ringed Abrolhos islands, perhaps seeing humpback whales along the way.

Porto Seguro is well connected to Salvador, as well as to Rio, São Paulo and Belo Horizonte from where you can connect to other itineraries in this book or to a flight home.

# When
## to go

## Climate

Bahia enjoys a warm, humid tropical climate, with year-round temperatures in the high 20s and low 30s, cooled by perennial sea breezes. It's possible to visit all year round. Temperatures are coolest between April and November. Rains fall most heavily between April and July, when the coast can be swathed in cloud for days on end. While it's always possible to find an empty beach, Bahia, like the rest of Brazil, can be busy over the peak Brazilian holiday times (mid-December to early January and the 10 days on and around Carnival – beginning the weekend before Shrove Tuesday – and in July.

## Festivals

Carnaval dates depend on the ecclesiastical calendar and so vary from year to year. The party begins on the Friday afternoon before Shrove Tuesday, officially ending on Ash Wednesday and unofficially on the following Sunday. The biggest parties are in Salvador (whose carnival is second only to Rio's in size) and on the beach in Porto Seguro.

**Carnival** dates
**2017** 23 February-1 March
**2018** 8-14 February
**2019** 28 February-6 March

**Weather** Salvador

| January | February | March | April | May | June |
|---|---|---|---|---|---|
| 30°C | 30°C | 30°C | 28°C | 28°C | 27°C |
| 24°C | 24°C | 24°C | 24°C | 23°C | 22°C |
| 88mm | 125mm | 160mm | 312mm | 313mm | 233mm |

| July | August | September | October | November | December |
|---|---|---|---|---|---|
| 26°C | 26°C | 27°C | 28°C | 29°C | 29°C |
| 21°C | 21°C | 21°C | 22°C | 23°C | 23°C |
| 205mm | 129mm | 94mm | 108mm | 125mm | 110mm |

## January

**Reveillon** (New Year's Eve). Big parties in Salvador and Porto Seguro and supermodel holiday season in Trancoso.

**Procissão de Nosso Senhor dos Navegantes**, Salvador, Bahia. A big procession and a key event of the *candomblé* calendar.

**Festa do Bonfim**, see www.bahia-online.net/festas.

## February

**Festa de Yemanjá**, Rio Vermelho, Salvador, Bahia. Dedicated to the candomblé orixá (spirit) of the sea and a great place to hear authentic live Bahian bands.

## August

**Festa da Nossa Senhora D'Ajuda**, Arraial d'Ajuda, Bahia. Festivals and processions celebrating the town's patron saint.

## October

**Carnoporto**, Porto Seguro's huge out-of-season carnival with all the top cheesy Bahian bands and big crowds. See www.axemoifolia.com.br.

# What to do

from diving and surfing to whitewater rafting

## Birdwatching

Almost a fifth of the world's bird species are Brazilian. The country is home to some 1750 species, of which 218 are endemic and 165 globally threatened, both the highest numbers of any country in the world. Many of these endemics live in the Atlantic coastal rainforests of which there are large stretches in Bahia around Itacaré and Porto Seguro. Brazil also has the largest number of globally threatened birds: 120 of 1212 worldwide. This is accounted for partly by the numbers of critically threatened habitats that include the Atlantic coastal rainforest, which recently lost the Alagoas currassow, and the *caatinga*, which has lost Spix's macaw, the blue parrot which starred in the film *Rio*, which once lived in the Bahian *sertão*.

Bahia is superb for birdwatching, with more than 20 sites designated as of global importance by **Birdlife International** (www.birdlife.org). Many of the rarest and most spectacular birds in the world can be seen on a visit to the state. They include blue Lear's macaws which nest around Canudos, harpy eagles which have recently been found in the Serra Bonita reserve and numerous endemic Atlantic coastal species. Birdwatching trips can be organized with northeastern Brazil specialist bird guide **Ciró Albano** (www.nebrazilbirding.com).

See page 125 for a list of international companies offering Brazilian birdwatching and wildlife tours. The best time for birding is September-October as it is quiet, relatively dry and flights are cheapest. Two comprehensive websites are **www.worldtwitch.com** and **www.camacdonald.com**.

## Caving

There are some wonderful cave systems in Brazil, and Ibama has a programme for the protection of the national speleological heritage. National parks such as Chapada Diamantina have easy access for the casual visitor.

For more information, contact agencies in Bahia like **Orbita** (see page 76) or any listed in Lençóis in the Chapada Diamantina (see page 103).

## Climbing and hill walking

There is excellent hiking, scrambling and climbing in the Chapada Diamantina, all easily organized through agencies in Lençóis village (see page 103). Rugged rainforest hikes in the Monte Pascoal national park on the southern Atlantic coast can be arranged through **Mata N'ativa** or **Portomondo** (see page 95).

**Planning your trip** What to do • 13

## Cycling and mountain biking

Brazil is well suited to cycling, both on and off-road and adventure bike trips are easily organized in the forest trails around Trancoso and Itacaré. On main roads, keep on the lookout for motor vehicles, as cyclists are very much treated as second-class citizens. Also note that when cycling on the northeastern coast you may encounter strong winds which will hamper your progress. There are endless roads and tracks suitable for mountain biking, and there are many clubs in major cities which organize group rides, activities and competitions.

## Diving and snorkelling

The Abrolhos archipelago off the coast of Bahia state in northeastern Brazil has huge brain corals and, in the Brazilian summer, humpback whale sightings are pretty much guaranteed. There's good snorkelling over the reefs of southern Bahia, particularly around Santo André, though you will need to take a boat trip to reach the best of them.

Cave diving can be practised in many underwater grottoes such as those in Chapada Diamantina.

## Surfing

There are good conditions all along the coast. Brazilians love to surf and are well-represented in international competitions, which are frequently held on the beaches near Itacaré in Bahia, the most sought after surf destination in the state, and one of the most coveted in Brazil. Many tour companies offer surf trips or lessons; contact **Órbita**, **Mata N'ativa** or **Portomondo** for details (see pages 76 and 95).

## Wind and kitesurfing

Northern Bahia has gentle kite and windsurfing, but it can't compare with destinations further north in Brazil's Ceará and Maranhão states.

# Where
## to stay

*from pensões to pousadas*

There is a good range of accommodation options in Bahia. An *albergue* or hostel offers the cheapest option. These have dormitory beds and single and double rooms. Many are part of **Hostelling International (HI)** ⓘ *www.hihostels.com*; **Hostel World** ⓘ *www.hostelworld.com*, **Hostel Bookers** ⓘ *www.hostelbookers.com*, and **Hostel.com** ⓘ *www.hostel.com*, are all useful portals. **Hostel Trail Latin America** ⓘ *T0131-208 0007 (UK), www.hosteltrail.com*, managed from their hostel in Popayan, is an online network of hotels and tour companies in South America. A *pensão* is either a cheap guesthouse or a household that rents out some rooms.

**Pousadas**
A *pousada* is either a bed-and-breakfast, often small and family-run, or a sophisticated and often charming small hotel. A *hotel* is as it is anywhere else in the world, operating according to the international star system, although five-star hotels are not price controlled and hotels in any category are not always of the standard of their star equivalent in the USA, Canada or Europe. Many of the older hotels can be cheaper than hostels. Usually accommodation prices include a breakfast of rolls, ham, cheese, cakes and fruit with coffee and juice; there is no reduction if you don't eat it. Rooms vary too. Normally an *apartamento* is a room with separate living and sleeping areas and sometimes cooking facilities. A *quarto* is a standard room; *com banheiro* is en suite; and *sem banheiro* is with shared bathroom. Finally there are the *motels*. These should not be confused

---

## Price codes

| Where to stay | Restaurants |
|---|---|
| $$$$ over US$150 | $$$ over US$12 |
| $$$ US$66-150 | $$ US$7-12 |
| $$ US$30-65 | $ US$6 and under |
| $ under US$30 | |

Price of a double room in high season, including taxes.

Price for a two-course meal for one person, excluding drinks or service charge.

with their US counterpart: motels are used by guests not intending to sleep; there is no stigma attached and they usually offer good value (the rate for a full night is called the '*pernoite*'), however the decor can be a little garish.

It's essential to book accommodation at peak times.

Hidden Pousadas Brazil ⓘ *www.hiddenpousadasbrazil.com*, offers a range of the best *pousadas*.

### Luxury accommodation
Much of the best private accommodation sector can be booked through operators. Angatu ⓘ *www.angatu.com*, offers bespoke trips. Matuete ⓘ *www. matuete.com*, has a range of luxurious properties and tours.

### Camping
Those with an international camping card pay only half the rate of a non-member at Camping Clube do Brasil sites ⓘ *www.campingclube.com.br*. Membership of the club itself is expensive: US$70 for six months. It may be difficult to get into some Camping Clube campsites during high season (January to February). Private campsites charge about US$6-8 per person. For those on a very low budget and in isolated areas where there is no campsite available, it's usually possible to stay at service stations. They have shower facilities, watchmen and food; some have dormitories. There are also various municipal sites. Campsites tend to be some distance from public transport routes and are better suited to people with their own car. Wild camping is generally difficult and dangerous. Never camp at the side of a road; this is very risky.

### Quality hotel associations
The better international hotel associations have members in Brazil. These include: Small Luxury Hotels of the World ⓘ *www.slh.com*; the Leading Hotels of the World ⓘ *www.lhw.com*; the Leading Small Hotels of the World ⓘ *www. leadingsmallhotelsoftheworld.com*; Great Small Hotels ⓘ *www.greatsmallhotels. com*; and the French group Relais et Chateaux ⓘ *www.relaischateaux.com*, which also includes restaurants.

The Brazilian equivalent of these associations are Hidden Pousadas Brazil ⓘ *www.hiddenpousadasbrazil.com*, and their associate, the Roteiros de Charme ⓘ *www.roteirosdecharme.com.br*. Membership of these groups pretty much guarantees quality, but it is by no means comprehensive.

**Online travel agencies (OTAs)**

Services like www.tripadvisor.com and OTAs associated with them, such as www.hotels.com, www.expedia.com and www.venere.com, are well worth using for both reviews and for booking ahead. Hotels booked through an OTA can be up to 50% cheaper than the rack rate. Similar sites operate for hostels (though discounts are far less considerable). They include the Hostelling International site, www.hihostels.com, www.hostelbookers.com, www. hostels.com and www.hostelworld.com.

## Improve your travel photography

Taking pictures is a highlight for many travellers, yet too often the results turn out to be disappointing. Steve Davey, author of Footprint's *Travel Photography*, sets out his top rules for coming home with pictures you can be proud of.

### Before you go

Don't waste precious travelling time and do your research before you leave. Find out what festivals or events might be happening or which day the weekly market takes place, and search online image sites such as Flickr to see whether places are best shot at the beginning or end of the day, and what vantage points you should consider.

### Get up early

The quality of the light will be better in the few hours after sunrise and again before sunset – especially in the tropics when the sun will be harsh and unforgiving in the middle of the day. Sometimes seeing the sunrise is a part of the whole travel experience: sleep in and you will miss more than just photographs.

### Stop and think

Don't just click away without any thought. Pause for a few seconds before raising the camera and ask yourself what you are trying to show with your photograph. Think about what things you need to include in the frame to convey this meaning. Be prepared to move around your subject to get the best angle. Knowing the point of your picture is the first step to making sure that the person looking at the picture will know it too.

### Compose your picture

Avoid simply dumping your subject in the centre of the frame every time you take a picture. If you compose with it to one side, then your picture can look more balanced. This will also allow you to show a significant background and make the picture more meaningful. A good rule of thumb is to place your subject or any significant detail a third of the way into the frame; facing into the frame not out of it.

This rule also works for landscapes. Compose with the horizon two-thirds of the way up the frame if the foreground is the most interesting part of the picture; one-third of the way up if the sky is more striking.

Don't get hung up with this so-called Rule of Thirds, though. Exaggerate it by pushing your subject out to the edge of the frame if it makes a more interesting picture; or if the sky is dull in a landscape, try cropping with the horizon near the very top of the frame.

### Fill the frame

If you are going to focus on a detail or even a person's face in a close-up portrait, then be bold and make sure that you fill the frame. This is often a case of physically getting in close. You can use a telephoto setting on a zoom lens but this can lead to pictures looking quite flat; moving in close is a lot more fun!

### Interact with people

If you want to shoot evocative portraits then it is vital to approach people and seek permission in some way, even if it is just by smiling at someone. Spend a little time with them and they are likely to relax and look less stiff and formal. Action portraits where people are doing something, or environmental portraits, where they are set against a significant background, are a good way to achieve relaxed portraits. Interacting is a good way to find out more about people and their lives, creating memories as well as photographs.

### Focus carefully

Your camera can focus quicker than you, but it doesn't know which part of the picture you want to be in focus. If your camera is using the centre focus sensor then move the camera so it is over the subject and half press the button, then, holding it down, recompose the picture. This will lock the focus. Take the now correctly focused picture when you are ready.

Another technique for accurate focusing is to move the active sensor over your subject. Some cameras with touch-sensitive screens allow you to do this by simply clicking on the subject.

### Leave light in the sky

Most good night photography is actually taken at dusk when there is some light and colour left in the sky; any lit portions of the picture will balance with the sky and any ambient lighting. There is only a very small window when this will happen, so get into position early, be prepared and keep shooting and reviewing the results. You can take pictures after this time, but avoid shots of tall towers in an inky black sky; crop in close on lit areas to fill the frame.

### Bring it home safely

Digital images are inherently ephemeral: they can be deleted or corrupted in a heartbeat. The good news though is they can be copied just as easily. Wherever you travel, you should have a backup strategy. Cloud backups are popular, but make sure that you will have access to fast enough Wi-Fi. If you use RAW format, then you will need some sort of physical back-up. If you don't travel with a laptop or tablet, then you can buy a backup drive that will copy directly from memory cards.

*Recently updated and available in both digital and print formats, Footprint's Travel Photography by Steve Davey covers everything you need to know about travelling with a camera, including simple post-processing. More information is available at www.footprinttravelguides.com*

# Food
## & drink

*from a* chope *with* churrasco *to a* pinga *with* pesticos

## Food

While Brazil has some of the best fine dining restaurants in Latin America and cooking has greatly improved over the last decade, everyday Brazilian cuisine can be stolid. Mains are generally heavy, meaty and unspiced. Desserts are often very sweet. The Brazilian staple meal generally consists of a cut of fried or barbecued meat, chicken or fish accompanied by rice, black or South American broad beans and an unseasoned salad of lettuce, grated carrot, tomato and beetroot. Condiments consist of weak chilli sauce, olive oil, salt and pepper and vinegar.

The national dish – which is associated with Rio – is a heavy campfire stew called *feijoada*, made by throwing jerked beef, smoked sausage, tongue and salt pork into a pot with lots of fat and beans and stewing it for hours. The resulting stew is sprinkled with fried *farofa* (manioc flour) and served with *couve* (kale) and slices of orange. The meal is washed down with *cachaça* (sugar cane rum). Most restaurants serve the *feijoada completa* for Saturday lunch (up until about 1630). Come with a very empty stomach.

Brazil's other national dish is mixed grilled meat or *churrasco*, served in vast portions off the spit by legions of rushing waiters, and accompanied by a buffet of salads, beans and mashed vegetables. *Churrascos* are served in *churrascarias* or *rodízios*. The meat is generally excellent, especially in the best *churascarias*, and the portions are unlimited, offering good value for camel-stomached carnivores able to eat one meal a day.

In remembrance of Portugal, but bizarrely for a tropical country replete with fish, Brazil is also the world's largest consumer of cod, pulled from the cold north Atlantic, salted and served in watery slabs or little balls as *bacalhau* (an appetizer/bar snack) or *petisco*. Other national *petiscos* include *kibe* (a deep-fried or baked mince with onion, mint and flour), *coxinha* (deep-fried chicken or meat in dough), *empadas* (baked puff-pastry patties with prawns, chicken, heart of palm or meat), and *tortas* (little pies with the same ingredients). When served in bakeries, *padarias* or snack bars these are collectively referred to as *salgadinhos* (savouries).

**Bahia** offers an African-infused, welcome break from meat, rice and beans further south, with a variety of seafood dishes. Unlike most Brazilians, Bahians have discovered sauces, pepper and chilli. The most famous Bahian dish is *moqueca* (fresh fish cooked slowly with prawns in *dendê* palm oil, coconut milk, garlic, tomatoes, cilantro and chili pepper). Other Bahian dishes include *vatapá* and *caruaru* (pastes made from prawns, nuts, bread, coconut milk and *dendê* oil), *xinxim de galinha* (a rich, spicy chicken stew, best without *dendê* oil), and *acarajé* (black-eyed peas or beans squashed into a ball, deep-fried in *dendê* oil and served split in half, stuffed with *vatapá* or *caruaru* and seasoned with chilli).

There are myriad unusual, delicious fruits in Brazil, many with unique flavours. They include the pungent, sweet *cupuaçu*, which makes delicious cakes, the tart *camu-camu*, a large glass of which holds a gram of vitamin C, and *açaí* – a dark and highly nutritious berry from a *várzea* (seasonally flooded forest) palm tree, common in the Amazon. *Açaí* berries are often served as a frozen paste, garnished with *xarope* (syrup) and sprinkled with *guaraná* (a ground seed, also from the Amazon, which has stimulant effects similar to caffeine). Brazil also produces some of the world's best mangoes, papayas, bananas and custard apples, all of which come in a variety of flavours and sizes.

### Eating cheaply

The cheapest dish is the *prato feito* or *sortido*, an excellent-value set menu usually comprising meat/chicken/fish, beans, rice, chips and salad. The *prato comercial* is similar but rather better and a bit more expensive. Portions are usually large enough for two and come with two plates. If you are on your own, you could ask for an *embalagem* (doggy bag) or a *marmita* (takeaway) and offer it to a person with no food (many Brazilians do). Many restaurants serve *comida por kilo* buffets where you serve yourself and pay for the weight of food on your plate. This is generally good value and is a good option for vegetarians. *Lanchonetes* and *padarias* (diners and bakeries) are good for cheap eats, usually serving *prato feitos*, *salgadinhos*, excellent juices and other snacks.

The main meal is usually taken in the middle of the day; cheap restaurants tend not to be open in the evening.

## Drink

The national liquor is *cachaça* (also known as *pinga*), which is made from sugar cane, and ranging from cheap supermarket and service-station firewater, to boutique distillery and connoisseur labels. Mixed with fruit juice, sugar and crushed ice, *cachaça* becomes the principal element in a *batida*, a refreshing but deceptively powerful drink. Served with pulped lime or other fruit, mountains of sugar and smashed ice it becomes the world's favourite party cocktail, caipirinha. A less potent caipirinha made with vodka is called a *caipiroska* and with sake a *saikirinha* or *caipisake*.

Some genuine Scotch whisky brands are bottled in Brazil. They are far cheaper even than duty free; Teacher's is the best. Locally made and cheap gin, vermouth and Campari are pretty much as good as their US and European counterparts.

Wine is becoming increasingly popular and Brazil is the third most important wine producer in South America. The wine industry is mainly concentrated in the south of the country. Reasonable national table wines include Château d'Argent, Château Duvalier, Almadén, Dreher, Preciosa and more respectable Bernard Taillan, Marjolet from Cabernet grapes, and the Moselle-type white Zahringer. There are some interesting sparkling wines in the Italian spumante style (the best is Casa Valduga Brut Premium Sparkling Wine), and Brazil produces still wines using many international and imported varieties. The best bottle of red is probably the Boscato Reserva Cabernet Sauvignon, but it's expensive (at around US$20 a bottle); you'll get far higher quality and better value buying Portuguese, Argentine or Chilean wines in Brazil.

Brazilian beer is generally lager, served ice-cold. Draught beer is called *chope* or *chopp* (after the German Schoppen, and pronounced 'shoppi'). There are various national brands of bottled beers, which include Brahma, Skol, Cerpa, Antartica and the best Itaipava and Bohemia. There are black beers too, notably Xingu. They tend to be sweet. The best beer is from the German breweries in Rio Grande do Sul and is available only there.

Brazil's fruits are used to make fruit juices or *sucos*, which come in a delicious variety, unrivalled anywhere in the world. *Açai acerola*, *caju* (cashew), *pitanga*, *goiaba* (guava), *genipapo*, *graviola* (*chirimoya*), *maracujá* (passion fruit), *sapoti*, *umbu* and *tamarindo* are a few of the best. *Vitaminas* are thick fruit or vegetable drinks with milk. *Caldo de cana* is sugar-cane juice, sometimes mixed with ice. *Água de côco* or *côco verde* is coconut water served straight from a chilled, fresh, green coconut. The best known of many local soft drinks is *guaraná*, which is a very popular carbonated fruit drink, completely unrelated to the Amazon nut. The best variety is *guaraná antarctica*. Coffee is ubiquitous and good tea entirely absent.

# Menu reader

## A
**água de côco** coconut water
**arroz doce** rice pudding

## B
**bacalhau** salt cod
**bauru** sandwich made with melted cheese, roast beef and tomatoes

## C
**cachaça** sugar cane rum
**caipirinha** cocktail of crushed fruit (usually limes), *cachaça* and lots of sugar and ice
**caju** cashew
**caldo de cana** sugar cane juice
**caldo de feijão** bean soup
**chope/chopp** draught beer
**churrasco** mixed grilled meat
**churrasqueira** restaurant serving all-you-can-eat barbecued meat
**côco verde** coconut water served from a chilled, fresh, green coconut
**comida por kilo** pay-by-weight food
**coxinha** shredded chicken or other meat covered in dough and breadcrumbs and deep fried
**curau** custard flan-type dessert made with maize

## E
**empadas** or **empadinhas** puff-pastries with prawns, meat or palm hearts

## F
**farofa** fried cassava flour
**feijoada** hearty stew of black beans, sausages and pork
**frango churrasco** grilled chicken

## K
**kibe a petisco** deep-fried or baked mince with onion, mint and flour

## M
**mandioca frita** fried manioc root
**maracujá** passion fruit
**misto quente** toasted ham and cheese sandwich
**moqueca** seafood stew cooked with coconut and palm oil

## P/Q
**padaria** bakery
**palmito** palm heart
**pamonha** paste of milk and corn boiled in a corn husk
**pão de queijo** a roll made with cheese
**pastéis** deep-fried pastries filled with cheese, minced beef, or palm heart
**peixe** fish
**petisco** a tapas-style snack
**picanha** rump, a popular cut of beef
**pinga** sugar cane rum
**prato feito/prato comercial** set meal
**queijo** cheese

## R
**requeijão** ricotta-like cream cheese
**roupa velha** literally meaning 'old clothes', a dish of shredded dried meat served with rice *mandiocas*

## S
**salgadinhos** savoury snacks such as *empadas* and *tortas*
**sortido** inexpensive set meal
**suco** fruit juice

## T
**tortas** small pies filled with prawns, chicken, palm hearts or meat

## V
**vatapá** fish and prawn stew cooked in a creamy peanut sauce
**vitaminas** fruit or veg drinks with milk

# Salvador

Salvador is the capital not just of Bahia but of African Brazil. The country's African heritage is at its strongest here – in the ubiquitous *Orixá* spirit gods and goddesses, the carnival rhythms of the drum troupe orchestras of Ilê Aiyê and Olodum, the rich spicy cooking, the rituals of *candomblé* (Brazil's equivalent of *santeria*) and in the martial art ballet of capoeira. You will see the latter being performed on Salvador's beaches and in the squares and cobbled streets of the city's historical centre, the Pelourinho. The Pelourinho is also home to one of the most impressive collections of colonial architecture in South America. There are myriad baroque churches here. Some, like the Convento do São Francisco, have interiors covered with tons of gold plate. Others, like Nossa Senhora do Rosário, are decorated with statues of black saints and art that celebrates African Brazilian culture.

The city is famous for its frenetic carnival which, unlike Rio's, takes place in the streets to the pounding rhythms of *axé* music. The crowds are overwhelming and move like a human wave.

# Essential Salvador

## Finding your feet

Flights arrive at **Luís Eduardo Magalhães Airport**, 28 km east of the centre. Buses link the airport with the city. **Aeroporto** (Linha S002-00) buses run from the airport to the historic centre (Praça da Sé) every 30 minutes, US$0.85, via Rio Vermelho, Barra and the city beaches. Fixed-rate taxis go to Barra and the centre for around US$30. Ordinary taxis cost US$25.

Interstate buses arrive at the *rodoviária*, 5 km east of the centre, near **Iguatemi Shopping Centre**. There are regular bus services to the centre, Campo Grande, Barra and Rio Vermelho (marked Praça da Sé/Centro). A taxi to the centre costs around US$25.

The main ferry dock, principally for car ferries although also for catamarans and passenger boats, is the **Marítimo de São Joaquim**, on Avenida Oscar Pontes 1051. Salvador's other boat terminal, the **Terminal Marítimo de Mercado Modelo** or **Terminal Marítimo Turistico**, is smaller and for passenger-only boats. It lies opposite Mercado Modelo, five minutes' walk from the historic centre. See also Transport, page 54.

## Getting around

The centre of the city is divided into two levels, the **Cidade Alta** (Upper City) with the historic centre and Pelourinho, and the **Cidade Baixa** (Lower City), the commercial and docks district. The two levels are connected by a series of steep hills called *ladeiras*. The easiest way to go from one level to the other is by the **Lacerda Lift**, which connects Praça Municipal (Tomé de Sousa) in the Upper City with Praça Cairu and the famous **Mercado Modelo** market. The **Plano Inclinado Gonçalves** funicular railway leaves from behind the cathedral and runs to Comércio, the commercial district of the lower city near the market. The **Plano Inclinado do Pilar** funicular runs from next to the Pousada do Pilar in Santo Antonio to the Comércio.

Roads between the centre, Barra, the Atlantic suburbs and the Itapagipe Peninsula north of the centre are easy to follow and well served by public transport; see Bus, page 55.

## Orientation

The city is built on a broad peninsula and is at the mouth of the Baía de Todos os Santos. The commercial district of the city and its port are on the sheltered western side of the peninsula; residential districts and beaches are on the open Atlantic side. Barra lies at the point of the peninsula.

## Safety

There is a lot of paranoia about safety in Salvador but as long you follow common sense and a few rules they should be fine. The civil police are helpful and Barra, the Pelourinho and the old part of the city are well lit at night with a strong police presence. The Pelourinho area is generally safe: there's some pickpocketing, but muggings are rare (usually occurring late at night). Be vigilant and do not use the Lacerda Lift and funiculars at night and do not go to the Comercio area of the Lower City after dark. Only venture into favelas on a tour or with a trustworthy local friend. Women can receive unwelcome amounts of attention, especially during **Carnaval**.

## When to go

Summer (October to March) is hot, and it remains warm during the winter months (April to September). April to July are the wettest months, but there is no dry season.

## Immigration

**Polícia Federal**, Avenida O Pontes 339, Aterro de Água de Meninos, Lower City, T071-3319 6082. Open 1000-1600. For extensions of entry permits show an outward ticket or sufficient funds for your stay, visa extension US$9.

the baroque and rococo, capoiera-drum beating heart of old Salvador

Most of the interesting sights in Salvador (population 3.2 million) are concentrated in the Centro Histórico in the Cidade Alta (Upper City). This is where the Portuguese founded the first capital of Brazil in November 1549. The entire 2-km stretch between the Praça Municipal in the south and the Carmelite churches (Carmo) in the north is a UNESCO World Heritage Site.

The colonial houses in this area are painted in pastel colours, and many have been converted into restaurants, small hotels or bars, whose tables spill out onto the patios behind the houses; they host live music several times a week. The entire area proliferates with handicraft shops, artist ateliers and African-Brazilian cultural centres.

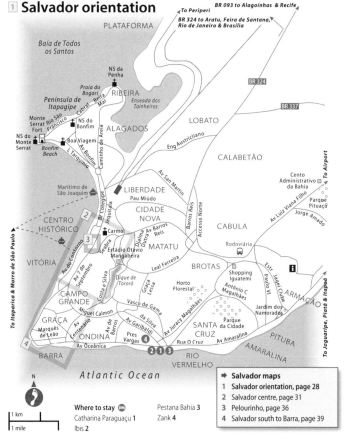

### 1 Salvador orientation

**Where to stay** 🛏
Catharina Paraguaçu 1
Ibis 2
Pestana Bahia 3
Zank 4

➡ **Salvador maps**
1 Salvador orientation, page 28
2 Salvador centre, page 31
3 Pelourinho, page 36
4 Salvador south to Barra, page 39

**Note**  Most of the churches and museums in the Centro Histórico prohibit the taking of pictures; even without a flash.

## Praça Municipal (Tomé de Souza) and the Praça da Sé

These adjacent squares (connected by the Rua da Misericórdia), link with neighbouring Terreiro de Jesus (Praça 15 de Novembro) to form an almost entirely pedestrianized zone. A decade ago this area was seedy, but it has been tidied up in recent years. The streets are lined with stores and stalls selling arts and crafts, music and souvenirs, and there are plenty of places for snacks and refreshments.

The **Praça Municipal** is the oldest part of Salvador – where the first governor, Thomé de Souza, built the first administrative buildings and churches (after unceremoniously clearing an indigenous Tupinambá village from the site). A statue of the soldier stands on a plinth gazing wistfully out to sea at the southern end of the *praça*. From here the city grew in a bewildering panoply of architectural styles, many of which can be seen around the square.

**Tip...**
There are wonderful views over the bay from Elevador Lacerda in Cidade Alta.

Dominating the view are the neoclassical columns of the former council chamber (1660), now the **Paço Municipal** ① *Praça Municipal s/n, T071-3176 4200, Tue-Sat 0930-1700, free*, and the imposing **Palácio Rio Branco** ① *Praça Municipal s/n, T071-3176 4200, Tue-Sat 0930-1700, free*. Like many of Brazil's opulent buildings, this was built in homage to the French for the state-governor, in 1918. The palace now houses municipal offices. On the western side of the square is the star of many postcards: the huge, art deco **Elevador Lacerda** ① *US$0.03*, which whisks people from the Cidade Alta to the Cidade Baixa, 70 m below, in seconds. It was built in the late 1920s to replace an old hydraulic lift, which in turn replaced the original rope and pulley system first installed by the Jesuits.

Heading north from the *praça*, Rua da Misericórdia runs past the church of **Santa Casa Misericórdia** ① *T071-3322 7666, open by arrangement 0800-1700*, (1695), with its high altar and beautiful painted *azulejos* (tiles), to **Praça da Sé**. This is one of central Salvador's most attractive squares, decorated with modernist fountains, shaded by mimosa and flamboyant trees and lined with stately buildings, many of which house smart shops or European-style cafés. Look out for the **Cruz Caída** (Fallen Cross), a sculpture of a fallen and broken crucifix by one of Latin America's foremost sculptors, Mário Cravo Junior (www.cravo.art.br). It is dedicated to the old Igreja da Sé (cathedral), which was pulled down in 1930, together with an entire street of 18th- and early 19th-century townhouses, to make way for the now defunct tramline. Some of the cathedral's foundations have been uncovered and lie bare near the Cruz, covered in wild flowers.

Immediately opposite the Cruz Caída is the **Memorial da Baiana do Acarajé** ① *Praça da Sé s/n, Mon-Fri 0900-1200 and 1400-1800, US$3*, a museum and cultural centre telling the story of the *Baianas* (the Bahian women who lead the **Lavagem do Bonfim** parade and who participate in **Carnaval** throughout Brazil wearing traditional large swirling dresses). There are panels, ritual objects and historic photographs and the café next door serves Bahian snacks and has a small souvenir shop.

## Terreiro de Jesus (Praça 15 de Novembro)

Immediately northeast of Praça da Sé, the Terreiro de Jesus is a large *praça* surrounded by handsome colonial townhouses and the bulk of the city's fabulous baroque churches. The square is the centre of tourist activity and bustles with bars, cafés and myriad souvenir stalls proffering everything from *acarajé* to *berimbaus*. It's particularly lively on Tuesday

## BACKGROUND
## Salvador

On 1 November 1501, All Saints' Day, the navigator Amérigo Vespucci discovered the bay and named it after the day of his arrival: Baía de Todos os Santos. The bay was one of the finest anchorages on the coast and became a favourite port of call for French, Spanish and Portuguese ships. However, when the Portuguese crown sent Martim Afonso to set up a permanent colony in Brazil, he favoured São Vicente in São Paulo.

It was not until nearly 50 years later that the bay's strategic importance was recognized. When the first governor general, Tomé de Sousa, arrived on 23 March 1549 to build a fortified city to protect Portugal's interest from constant threats of Dutch and French invasion, the bay was chosen as the place from which the new colony of Brazil was to be governed. Salvador was formally founded on 1 November 1549 and, despite a short-lived Dutch invasion in 1624, remained the capital of Brazil until 1763.

The city grew wealthy through the export of sugar and the import of African slaves to work on the plantations. By the 18th century, it was the most important city in the Portuguese empire after Lisbon, and ideally situated on the main trade routes of the New World. Its fortunes were further boosted by the discovery of diamonds in the interior. However, as the sugar industry declined, Rio de Janeiro became Brazil's principal city. Nevertheless, the city continued to play an influential part in the political and cultural life of the country.

### African presence
For three centuries, Salvador was the site of a thriving slave trade, with much of the workforce for the sugar cane and tobacco plantations coming from the west coast of Africa. Even today, Salvador is described as the most African city in the Western hemisphere, and the University of Bahia has the only choir in the Americas to sing in the Yoruba language. The influence permeates the city: food sold on the street is the same as in Senegal and Nigeria, the music is fused with pulsating African polyrhythms, and the pace of life is more relaxed than in other parts of the country.

### Modern Salvador
Salvador today is a fascinating mixture of old and modern, rich and poor, African and European, religious and profane. The city has 15 forts, 166 Catholic churches and 1000 *candomblé* temples. It remains a major port, exporting tropical fruit, cocoa, sisal, soya beans and petrochemical products. However, its most important industry is tourism, and it is the second largest tourist attraction in the country, after Rio.

Local government has done much to improve the fortunes of this once rundown, poor and dirty city. The once-forgotten Lower City, Ribeira and the Itapagipe Peninsula districts have received major facelifts. Major investments are being made by multinational firms in the automotive and petrochemical industries, principally in the Camaçari complex, 40 km from the city. The Bahian economy is currently the fastest growing in the country.

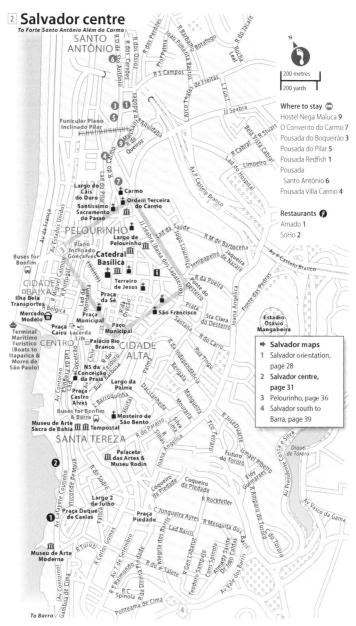

To Forte Santo Antônio Além do Carmo

SANTO ANTÔNIO

Funicular Plano Inclinado Pilar

Largo do Cais do Ouro
Santíssimo Sacramento do Passo
Carmo
Ordem Terceira do Carmo

PELOURINHO

Buses for Bonfim

Plano Inclinado Gonçalves
Largo de Pelourinho
Catedral Basílica

CIDADE BAIXA
Ilha Bela Transportes
Mercado Modelo
Terminal Marítimo Turístico (Boats to Itaparica & Morro de São Paulo)

Praça da Sé
Terreiro de Jesus
Praça Municipal
Paço Municipal
São Francisco
Sta Clara do Desterro

Praça Cairu
Lacerda Lift
Palácio Rio Branco

CENTRO   CIDADE ALTA

Praça Castro Alves

NS da Conceição da Praia
Largo da Palma

Buses for Bonfim

Mosteiro de São Bento

Museu de Arte Sacra de Bahia   Temporal

SANTA TEREZA

Palacete das Artes & Museu Rodin

Largo 2 de Julho
Praça Duque de Caxias
Praça Piedade

Museu de Arte Moderna

Estádio Otávio Mangabeira

Dique de Torôró

To Barra

N

200 metres
200 yards

### Where to stay

Hostel Nega Maluca 9
O Convento do Carmo 7
Pousada do Boqueirão 3
Pousada do Pilar 5
Pousada Redfish 1
Pousada Santo Antônio 6
Pousada Villa Carmo 4

### Restaurants

Amado 1
SoHo 2

→ Salvador maps
1  Salvador orientation, page 28
2  Salvador centre, page 31
3  Pelourinho, page 36
4  Salvador south to Barra, page 39

nights and weekends when there are shows or concerts (see Bars and clubs, page 48), and there are regular displays of **capoeira** – generally presented without joy and for the tourist dollar; if you stop to watch, you'll be expected to pay. Beware, too, of the persistent *Baianos* offering *fitas* (brightly coloured ribbons given as a good luck present), who swoop down like hawks on new arrivals. The streets that run off the south side of the Terreiro are frequented by drug dealers and beggars; this area is best avoided, especially after dark.

The Terreiro de Jesus takes its name from the 'Church of the Society of Jesus' (ie the Jesuits) that dominates it. It is now **Catedral Basílica** ⓘ *daily 0900-1200, 1400-1800, free*, devolving its ownership to the main body of the Catholic church in 1759, after the Jesuits were expelled from all Portuguese territories. The cathedral, whose construction dates from between 1657 and 1672, is one of the earliest examples of baroque in Brazil, a style that came to dominate in the 18th century and reached its full glory in Minas Gerais. The interior is magnificent: the vast vaulted ceiling and 12 side altars, in baroque and rococo, frame the main altar and are completely leafed in gold. This lavish display is offset by a series of Portuguese *azulejos* on in blue, white and yellow, which swirl together in a tapestry pattern.

The church is said to be built on the site of the original Jesuit chapel built by Padre Manuel da Nóbrega in the 16th century. Nóbrega was part of the crew on that came from Portugal with Brazil's first governor-general, Tomé de Sousa, arriving in Bahia on 29 March 1549. Together with Padre José de Anchieta, he founded many of the Jesuit seminaries and churches that later became the cities of modern Brazil, including Rio, Recife and São Paulo. **Antônio Vieira**, one of the greatest orators in Portuguese history and a campaigner for the protection of the indigenous Brazilians in the Amazon, preached some of his most famous sermons in the church. He died a sad and disgraced old man of nearly 90 in July 1697, condemned by the Dominican-run Inquisition and prohibited from either preaching or writing after being slanderously accused by his enemies of conniving in the murder of a colonial official. The cathedral also preserves the remains of Mem de Sá, the great and brutal Portuguese conquistador and third governor-general of Brazil, who perhaps more than anyone was responsible for the establishment of the Brazilian territories. He ruthlessly crushed the Tupinambá along the Bahian coast and, in liberating Rio from the French, he quelled an insurrection that threatened to overthrow the fledgling Brazilian colony. Note the interesting sculptures, particularly those on the altar of Saint Ursula in a huge chest carved from a trunk of Mata Atlântica *jacarandá*, encrusted with ivory, bone and turtle shell.

Across the square is the church of **São Pedro dos Clérigos** ⓘ *Praca 15 de Novembro, T071-3321 9183, Mon-Fri 0900-1200 and 1400-1800, free*, which is beautifully renovated. Alongside is the church of the early 19th-century **Ordem Terceira de São Domingos** ⓘ *Praca 15 de Novembro, T071-3242 4185, Mon-Fri 0900-1200, 1400-1700, free*, which has a beautiful 18th-century, painted wooden ceiling attributed to José Joaquim da Rocha, the father of the Bahian School – perhaps the first Brazilian school of art to adopt the contemporary European trompe l'oeil style – which used perspective to create the illusion of three-dimensions.

There are two interesting museums on the square, both housed in the former Jesuit College (and subsequent Bahian School of Medicine building). The **Museu Afro-Brasileiro (MAfro)** ⓘ *T071-3283 5540, www.mafro.ceao.ufba.br, Mon-Fri 0900-*

**Tip...**

The best way to get around is on the airport bus (see Essential Salvador, page 27), which runs between the historic centre, Barra and the beaches.

## ON THE ROAD
## Candomblé

*Candomblé* is a spiritual tradition that developed from religions brought over by Yoruba slaves from West Africa. It is focused on relationships with primordial spirits or *orixás* who are linked with natural phenomena and the calendar. The *orixás* are invoked in *terrelros* (temples). These can be elaborate, decorated halls, or simply someone's front room with tiny altars. Ceremonies are divided into two distinct parts. The first is when the *orixás* are invoked through different rhythms, songs and dances. Once the dancers have been possessed by the *orixá*, they are led off in a trance-like state to be changed into sacred, often very elaborate costumes, and come back to the ceremonial area in a triumphant procession in which each one dances separately for their deity. Overseeing the proceedings are *mães* or *pães de santo*, priestesses or priests.

*Candomblé* ceremonies may be seen by tourists, usually on Sundays and religious holidays – although many are just for show and not the real thing. The ceremonies can be very repetitive and usually last several hours, although you are not under pressure to remain for the duration. Appropriate and modest attire should be worn; visitors should not wear shorts, sleeveless vests or T-shirts. White clothing is preferred, black should not be worn especially if it is combined with red. Men and women are separated during the ceremonies, women always on the left, men on the right. No photography or sound recording is allowed. Most temples are closed during Lent, although each one has its own calendar. **Bahiatursa** (see page 42) has information about forthcoming ceremonies, but accurate information on authentic festivals is not always easy to come by.

*1730, Sat 1000-1700, US$1.50 for a joint ticket with MAE*, charts the history of Africans in Bahia. Between 1440-1640, Portugal monopolized the export of slaves from Africa and they were the last European country to abolish it. Over the course of 450 years, they were responsible for transporting more than 4.5 million Africans – some 40% of the total. There are countless exhibits, from both Brazil and the African continent itself, including fascinating ritual objects, musical instruments and textiles. Panels compare West African and Bahian *orixás* (deities) and, in a gallery all to themselves, are some beautiful wooden carved effigies by the artist Carybé (Hector Julio Páride Bernabó) who lived most of his life in Bahia. Carybé became famous with the *antropofagismo* movement, illustrating Mario de Andrade's *Macunaíma*, and won the prize as the best draughtsman in Brazil in 1955. He was later celebrated for his depictions of *candomblé* rituals and *orixás*.

In the basement of the same building, the **Museu de Arqueologia e Etnologia (MAE)** ⓘ *www.mae.ufba.br, Mon-Fri 0900-1700, US$1.50 for a joint ticket with MAfro*, houses indigenous Brazilian artefacts collected from all over Brazil over the centuries by the Jesuits, alongside archaeological discoveries from Bahia, such as stone tools, clay urns and rock art.

### Largo Cruzeiro de São Francisco and the Franciscan churches
Facing Terreiro de Jesus is the **Largo Cruzeiro de São Francisco**, crowded with souvenir stalls and dominated by a large wooden cross and the church and the modest façade of the convent of **São Francisco** ⓘ *Largo do Cruzeiro de São Francisco, T071-3322 6430, Mon-Sat*

*0800-1700, Sun 0800-1600, US$1.25.* The convent is the jewel in Salvador's baroque crown and one of the finest baroque churches in Latin America. The entrance leads to a sanctuary with another spectacular trompe l'oeil painting by **José Joaquim da Rocha** (1777) and to a set of cloisters decorated with minutely detailed and hand-painted azulejos; many are by the celebrated Portuguese artist Bartolomeu Antunes de Jesus. Each tile is based on illustrations to epigrams by Horace by the 17th-century Flemish humanist and teacher of Peter Paul Rubens, Otto Venius. "Quem e Rico? Quem nada ambiciona", proclaims one ('Who is rich? He who is ambitious for nothing'). The picture shows a man crowned from behind by a bare-breasted woman (representing glory) whilst simultaneously pushing away golden crowns (representing the trappings of aristocracy and establishment). It's hard not to regard this as irony when entering the church itself. It took 64 years to cover the interior with plated gold and iconic art; almost all of it paid for by that same establishment who had grown wealthy on the sugar trade. The irony is compounded by more *azulejos* around the altar showing scenes from St Francis' life, which was remarkable for the saint's Siddhartha-like rejection of his aristocratic birth right, in favour of mendicancy.

Irony aside, only a resolute inverted snob could fail to be transfixed by the artistry inside church. The main body of the church is the most opulent in Brazil, a vast, ornate exuberance of woodcarving in *jacarandá* depicting a riot of angels, animals, floral designs and saints, covered with some 800 kg of solid gold. It's easy to see that the work is by Africans and native Brazilians. Look out for the mask-like faces on the top right- and left-hand corners of the sacristy – an allusion to contemporaneous African art; and the cherubs below the pulpit and encrusted into the walls, whose genitals were hacked off by Portuguese far more prudish than those who carved their church. There are wonderful individual pieces too, including a beautiful sculpture of St Peter of Alcântara (venerated for his mystical visions attained in a state of painful ecstasy), agonisingly captured by the one of the fathers of Bahian baroque sculpture, Manoel Inácio da Costa. He was born in Camamu and known as 'Seis Dedos' (six fingers) to his contemporaries. And he chipped the figure from a single hunk of rainforest wood. Other unspecified statues are known to be by Bento dos Reis, born to African slaves and celebrated for the emotion he imparts to his figures. They may include a serene statue of the patron saint of African-Brazilians, the hermit Saint Benedict, born to Ethiopian slaves in Messina in Sicily in 1524 (beatified by Pope Benedict XIV in 1743), and invited to join the Franciscans order after suffering a racist jibe. He carries the Christ child in his arms. The names of the painters of the dozens of magnificent ceiling panels remain unknown.

Next door is the church of the **Ordem Terceira de São Francisco** ① *Ladeira da Ordem Terceira de São Francisco 3, T071-3321 6968, Mon-Sat 0800-1700, Sun 0800-1600, US$1.25,* (1703), with an intricate sandstone façade in the Spanish Churrigueresque style, an elaborate rococo form characterized by exuberant carving. It is one of only two such churches in the country and its carvings were completely covered over with plaster until the early 20th century, probably in protest against associations with Spain. There's a huge and intricately decorated altarpiece inside, a chapterhouse covered in striking images of the Order's most celebrated saints and a series of *azulejos* many depicting scenes of Lisbon before the devastating earthquake in 1755.

## The Pelourinho

The streets north of the Terreiro de Jesus, which run over a series of steep hills to the neighbourhood of Santo Antônio, are referred to as the Pelourinho. The area takes its name from the whipping post where the African slaves were auctioned off or punished by their Brazilian-

**Tip...**
Take a cab to and from the Pelourinho after dark.

Portuguese masters. Its steep cobbled streets are lined with brightly painted townhouses leading to little *praças* and always thronging with people. The bulk of the restaurants, small hotels and shops in the Centro Histórico are to be found here.

The Pelourinho's main thoroughfares run north off the Terreiro de Jesus. **Rua Alfredo Brito** (aka Portas do Carmo) and **Rua João de Deus** and the side streets that run off them are lined with three- or four-storey townhouses occupied by shops, restaurants and boutique hotels. Both descend in steep cobbles to the **Largo de Pelourinho**, a large sunny square watched over by one of Salvador's most important African-Brazilian monuments, the church of **Nossa Senhora do Rosário dos Pretos** ⓘ *Praça Jose Alencar s/n, Largo do Pelourinho, T071-3241 5781, Mon-Fri 0830-1800, Sat and Sun 0830-1500 and with African-Brazilian Mass every Tue at 1800, free*, built by former slaves over a period of 100 years, with what little financial resources they had. In colonial times, black Bahians were not even allowed to walk in front of the churches reserved for the white elite, let alone go inside them, and had to worship in their own building. The side altars honour black saints such as São Benedito (see Convento do São Francisco, above) and the painted ceiling and panels are by **Jose Joaquim da Rocha**. The overall effect is of simple tranquillity, in contrast to the busy opulence of the cathedral and the São Francisco church. The church remains a locus for black Bahian culture and has strong connections with *candomblé*. On Tuesdays, following a show by Olodum on the Pelourinho, there is an African-Brazilian Mass with singing accompanied by percussion from repiques, tambors and tamborins. Be sure to visit the haunting **Slave Cemetery** at the back of the building.

At the corner of Alfredo Brito and Largo do Pelourinho is a small museum dedicated to the work of Bahia's most famous author Jorge Amado, **Fundação Casa de Jorge Amado** ⓘ *Largo do Pelourinho s/n, T071-3321 0070, www.jorgeamado.org.br, Mon-Fri 0900-1800, Sat 1000-1600, free*. Amado was born and brought up around Ilhéus but spent much of his life in this house. The people of this part of Salvador provided the inspiration for the larger-than-life characters that populate some of his most famous novels including *Dona Flor e seus dois Maridos* (*Dona Flor and Her Two Husbands*, 1966). Information is in Portuguese only, but the walls of the museum café are covered with colourful copies of his book jackets in scores of languages, and all of his work is on sale.

Next door is the **Museu da Cidade** ⓘ *Praça Jose de Alencar 3, Largo do Pelourinho, T071-3321 1967, Tue-Fri 0900-1830, Sat 1300-1700, Sun 0900-1300, free, at the time of research the museum was temporarily closed for renovation and relocation*, in two adjacent 18th-century houses with exhibitions of arts and crafts, old photographs of the city, many fascinating objects from *candomblé* rituals and effigies of the *orixás*. A further room is devoted to the life and ouvre of the 19th-century abolitionist Antônio Frederico de Castro Alves (1847-1871).

Just around the corner from the Largo do Pelourinho is the **Museu Abelardo Rodrigues** ⓘ *Solar do Ferrão, R Gregório de Matos 45, T071-3320 9383, Tue-Sat 1300-1800, US$1.25*, which preserves one of the most important and impressive collections of religious art outside the São Paulo's Museu de Arte Sacra. It is housed in one of the Pelourinho's best-preserved and most stately 18th-century townhouses – once a Jesuit college – and showcases some impressive statuary, engravings, paintings and lavish monstrances from

Brazil, all over Latin America and the Far East. All were collected by the Pernambucan who gave the museum its name. There is also a smaller and less illustrious sacred art musuem, the **Museu de Arte Sacra da Bahia** (see page 40).

Below Nossa Senhora do Rosario dos Pretos is the **Museu Casa do Benin** ⓘ *R Padre Agostinho Gomes 17, Pelourinho, T071-3241 5679, casadobenin@yahoo.com.br, Mon-Fri 1200-*

### ③ Pelourinho

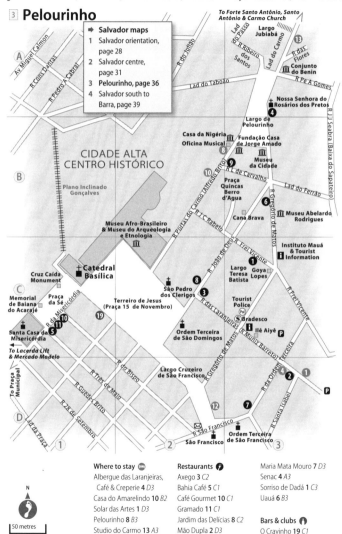

➡ **Salvador maps**
1 Salvador orientation, page 28
2 Salvador centre, page 31
3 Pelourinho, page 36
4 Salvador south to Barra, page 39

N

50 metres
50 yards

*1800, free*, which has displays of African-Brazilian crafts, photos and a video on Benin and Angola. It hosts exhibitions, dance shows and other artistic events. The **Casa da Nigéria** ① *R Alfredo de Brito 26, Pelourinho, T071-3328 3782*, offers a similar programme orientated more to Yoruba culture and has showcases of African and African-Brazilian arts and crafts, photographs and an important library. Yoruba language classes are available here and both cultural centres are important nexuses of African-Brazilian culture and society in Bahia.

## Morro do Carmo and Santo Antônio

The Ladeira do Carmo climbs up the steep **Morro do Carmo** hill running north from the Largo do Pelourinho, past the **Igreja do Santissimo Sacramento do Passo** and the steps that lead up to it (which were the setting for the city scenes in Anselmo Duarte's award-winning socio-political tragedy, *O Pagador de Promessas*, 'Keeper of the Promises'), to the **Largo do Carmo**. This little *praça*, at the junction of the Ladeira do Carmo and Rua Ribeiro dos Santos, is watched over by a series of Carmelite buildings. The most impressive is the **Igreja da Ordem Terceira do Carmo** ① *Morro do Carmo s/n, Mon-Sat 0800-1130, 1400-1730, Sun 1000-1200, US$1*, once a piece of striking baroque dating from 1709 but completely gutted in a fire 67 years later and restored in the 19th century. It is in a poor state of repair but houses one of the sacred art treasures of the city, a sculpture of Christ made in 1730 by Francisco Xavier 'O Cabra' Chagas ('the Goat'), a slave who had no formal training but who is celebrated by many locals as the Bahian Aleijadinho. Two thousand tiny rubies embedded in a mixture of whale oil, ox blood and banana resin give Christ's blood a ghostly, almost transparent appearance and the statue itself is so lifelike it appears almost to move. There is a small museum with a collection of ornate icons and period furniture. The adjacent **Igreja do Carmo** ① *Morro do Carmo s/n, Mon-Sat 0800-1200, 1400-1800, Sun 0800-1200, US$1*, a magnificent painted ceiling by the freed slave, José Teófilo de Jesus, while the **Convento do Carmo**, which served as a barracks for Dutch troops during the 1624 invasion, has been tastefully converted into Salvador's most luxurious hotel (see Where to stay, page 43).

Rua do Carmo continues to climb north from the Morro do Carmo into the neighbourhood of **Santo Antônio**, where dozens of the pretty colonial houses have been converted into tasteful boutique hotels and *pousadas*, the best of which have gorgeous bay views. The street eventually reaches the Barão do Triunfo (Largo de Santo Antônio), after about a kilometre. This handsome square (with barely a tourist in sight) is watched over by the hulking **Forte de Santo Antônio além do Carmo fortress** ① *Barão do Triunfo s/n, Santo Antônio, T071-3117 1488, Mon-Sat 0900-1200 and 1400-1700, US$4*, and another impressive church, the **Igreja de Santo Antônio Além do Carmo** ① *Largo Barão do Triunfo s/n, Santo Antônio, T071-3242 6463, Mon-Sat 0900-1200 and 1400-1730, free*. The fort dates from the last decade of the 17th century and is known locally as the Forte da Capoeira as it is home to half a dozen capoeira schools. It was restored at the turn of the 20th century and there are beautiful views over the bay from its walls.

## Cidade Baixa and Mercado Modelo

Salvador's Cidade Baixa (Lower City), which sits at the base of the cliff that runs from Santo Antônio in the north to Praça Municipal and Lacerda Lift in the south, was once as delightful and buzzing with life as the Pelourinho. Today, its handsome imperial and early republican 19th-century buildings, many of them covered in *azulejos*, are crumbled and cracked. Others have been pulled down and replaced with ugly concrete warehouses. There are numerous gorgeous baroque churches in a similar state of disrepair, most of them with doors permanently closed. With the exception of the ferry docks, the whole area is dangerous and down at heel – especially at night. However, there are plans for restoration. A big hotel group has apparently bought up one of the old colonial mansions, while musician Carlinhos Brown has established the **Museu du Ritmo** ① *R Torquato Bahia, 84 Edifício Mercado do Ouro, T071-3353 4333,* and the **International Centre for Black Music**, a complex built around a 1000-sq-m concert arena housed in a giant courtyard formed from the walls of a former colonial mansion house which once was home to the gold exchange. The museum has multimedia exhibits, a cinema, art gallery, school and recording studio on the site. Shows are advertized in the local press and on Carlinhos Brown's website: www.carlinhosbrown.com.br.

There are few other sights of interest. Bahia's best souvenir shopping is in the **Mercado Modelo** ① *Praça Visconde Cayru, Cidade Baixa, www.mercadomodelobahia.com.br, Tue-Sat 0900-1900, Sun 0900-1400.* This former customs house is thick with stalls selling everything from musical instruments to life-size sculptures hacked out of hunks of wood. Look out for the colourful handbags, made out of hundreds of can ring-pulls sewn together with fishing twine, and the *orixá* effigies and postcards. There are frequent capoeira shows between 1100 and 1300 on weekdays (you will have to pay to take pictures), occasional live music and numerous cafés and stalls selling Bahian cooking.

Further along the shore to the south is the striking, octaganol church of **Nossa Senhora da Conceição da Praia** ① *R Conceição da Praia at Av Contorno.* The church, which dates from 1736, was built in *lioz* marble in Portugal by Manuel Cardoso de Saldanha, disassembled bit by bit with the stones given numbers, then transported to Salvador and reconstructed. It has an unusual octagonal nave and diagonally set towers, modelled on churches in Portugal such as the Guarda cathedral. Inside it is magnificent, with a stunning ceiling painting of an Italianate panoply of saints gathered around the Madonna in glorious Renaissance perspective – the masterpiece of José Joaquim da Rocha.

## South of the centre

*modern Salvador, dotted with skyscraper apartment blocks*

South of the old centre towards the mouth of the bay is modern Salvador. Rua Chile leads to Praça Castro Alves, with its monument to the man who started the campaign that finally led to the abolition of slavery in 1888. Two streets lead out of this square: Avenida 7 de Setembro, busy with shops and street vendors selling everything imaginable; and, parallel to it, Rua Carlos Gomes.

**Mosteiro São Bento** ① *Av 7 de Setembro, T071-3322 4749, www.saobento.org, Mon-Fri 0900-1200 and 1300-1600, US$1.75,* another of Bahia's oldest religious buildings, dates from 1582 but was constructed much later. The cool, colonial spaces and cloistered garden are a welcome quiet space within the bustle of the city. The monastery was used as an arsenal by the Dutch during their occupation in 1624 and narrowly avoided going the way of much of colonial Rio and São Paulo in the 20th century, which were razed to the ground to make way for ugly modern skyscrapers. It houses a religious art museum with some 2000 priceless antiquities.

Just to the south is the **Palacete das Artes** ① *R da Graça 284, Graça, T071-3117 6986, www.palacetedasartes.ba.gov.br, Wed-Fri 1300-1900, Sat-Sun 1400-1900, free,* a small museum and cultural centre showing temporary exhibitions from Brazilian and notable Bahian artists, who in the past have included the likes of Mario Cravo Junior.

# 4 Salvador south to Barra

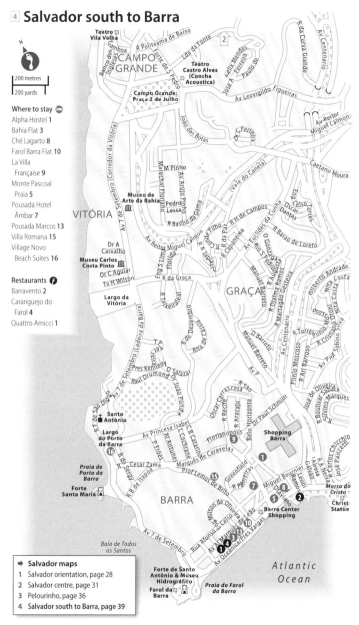

**N**

200 metres
200 yards

**Where to stay** 🛏
Alpha Hostel **1**
Bahia Flat **3**
Ché Lagarto **8**
Farol Barra Flat **10**
La Villa
  Française **9**
Monte Pascoal
  Praia **5**
Pousada Hotel
  Âmbar **7**
Pousada Marcos **13**
Villa Romana **15**
Village Novo
  Beach Suites **16**

**Restaurants** 🍴
Barravento **2**
Caranguejo do
  Farol **4**
Quattro Amicci **1**

**Museu de Arte Sacra da Bahia** ① *R do Sodré 276 off R Carlos Gomes, T071-3283 5600, Mon-Fri 1130-1700, US$2.50*, is in the 17th-century monastery and church of Santa Teresa d'Avila, at the bottom of the steep Ladeira de Santa Tereza. Many of the 400 carvings are from Europe, but there are some beautiful pieces by the artists who worked on the city's finest churches, such as Frei Agostinho de Piedade and José Joaquim da Rocha. Look out for the hauntingly life-like statue of Christ by the latter, carved from a piece of ivory and crucified on a *jacarandá* cross. Among the reliquaries of silver and gold is one made from gilded wood by Aleijadinho. The views from the patio, out over the Baía de Todos os Santos, are breathtaking and very little photographed. Opposite is **Tempostal** ① *R do Sodré 276, Tue-Fri 0900-1830, Sat and Sun 0900-1800*, a private museum of postcards.

Just inland near Campo Belo is the **Dique do Tororo** ① *Av Vasco de Gama*, a lake and leisure area decorated with 3-m-high *orixá* statues by the Bahian sculptor Tatti Moreno. There are large *candomblé* celebrations here at dawn on 2 February before the **Festa da Yemanjá**.

Further south, the **Museu de Arte Moderna and Solar do Unhão** ① *off Av Contorno, T071-3117 6139, www.mam.ba.gov.br, Tue-Fri 1300-1900, Sat 1300-2100, free*, is one of the finest modern art museums in northeastern Brazil. The collection includes work by most of Brazil's important artists, including Emiliano di Cavalcanti, the abstract painter Alfredo Volpi, social-expressionist Cândido Portinari and the co-founder of *antropofagismo*, Tarsila do Amaral; alongside pieces by Bahian artists such as Mario Cravo Junior, Carybé and the Franco-Bahian photographer Pierre Verger; and contemporary artists like Jose Bechara, Siron Franco and the photographer Mario Cravo Neto. The gallery is housed in the Solar do Unhão, which is itself an important historical monument. It sits right on the waterfront and was built in the 17th century initially as a sugar storage way station. It then became a mansion occupied by a series of influential Bahians over the following centuries, all of whom have left their mark on the building, from little chapels to beautiful painted *azulejos*. The gallery also hosts temporary exhibitions, has an arts cinema (www.saladearte.art.br) and a bar/café with live jazz on Saturdays from 1830. There are many restaurants nearby. The museum is close to a favela and there are occasional muggings particularly after dark; it's best to take a taxi.

Heading towards Porta da Barra, the **Museu de Arte da Bahia** ① *Av 7 de Setembro 2340, Vitória, Tue-Fri 1300-1900, Sat and Sun 1400-1900, free*, has interesting paintings by Bahian and Brazilian artists from the 18th to the early 20th century and a collection of 18th- and 19th-century furniture. A kilometre south of here is the **Museu Carlos Costa Pinto** ① *Av 7 de Setembro 2490, Vitória, www.museucostapinto.com.br, Mon and Wed-Sat 1430-1900, US$1.25*, in a modern house, with collections of crystal, porcelain, silver and furniture. It ostensibly has the world's only collection of *balangandãs* (slave charms and jewellery). The museum has a pleasant little garden café serving quiches, salads and cakes.

## Porto da Barra and the Atlantic beach suburbs

Barra is one of the most popular places to stay in Salvador. The strip from Porto da Barra as far as the Cristo at the end of the Farol da Barra beach has some of the city's liveliest cafés, restaurants, bars and clubs. A night out here, in nearby Campo Belo and in the exclusive restaurants and bars of the city's most upmarket venue, **Praça dos Tupinambas**, give an idea of how polarized Salvador society is. The clientele is much more

> **Tip...**
> Come to Barra for the best inner-city beaches in Salvador.

middle class than the Pelourhino; the music, food and conversation are more European and American and, in Brazil's African heart, there's hardly a black face in sight.

There are a few sights of moderate interest around Barra. The **Forte de Santo Antônio** and its famous lighthouse are right at the mouth of the bay where Baía de Todos os Santos and the South Atlantic Ocean meet. On the upper floors of the lighthouse, the **Museu Hidrográfico** ① *Tue-Sat 1300-1800, US$1.25*, has fine views of the coast. A promenade leads away from the fort, along the beach to the **Morro do Cristo** at the eastern end, which is crowned with a statue of Christ, arms outstretched over the bay. The statue is unremarkable in itself, but there are good views from the hill.

## Rio Vermelho and the ocean beaches

From Barra the beach road runs east through the beachfront suburbs of **Ondina** and **Rio Vermelho**. Confusingly, the road is known as both Avenida Oceânica and Avenida Presidente Vargas, and both have different numbering, making finding an address rather challenging. Rio Vermelho is the only suburb of interest. It has long been the home of many of Salvador's well-to-do artists and musicians and a centre for *candomblé*. Unlike the beachfront neighbourhoods around Barra, the clientele is a healthy mix of middle class and African-Brazilian.

There's a lively market with many little spit-and-sawdust bars, a handful of decent restaurants and small eateries serving some of the city's best *acarajé*. The area is busy at night, especially at weekends, and there are a number of venues playing traditional Bahian music. On 2 February the beach at Rio Vermelho is packed with *candomblé* pilgrims for the **Festa de Yemanjá**. To get here from the city centre, it is a 10-minute taxi ride (US$10-12) or a 20-minute bus journey on the airport–city centre bus. There are some good hotels nearby.

The next beaches along from Rio Vermelho are **Amaralina** and **Pituba**, neither of which are good for swimming but both of which have good surf and small fishing communities. Look out for *jangadas* (small rafts with sails peculiar to northeast Brazil) on the seashore. Bathing is better at **Jardim de Alah**, **Jaguaripe**, **Piatã** and **Itapoã**, all of which are fairly clean and have fluffy white sand and swaying coconut palms; any bus from Praça da Sé marked 'Aeroporto' or 'Itapoã' reaches the beaches in about an hour. Near Itapoã is the **Lagoa do Abaeté**, a deep freshwater lake surrounded by brilliant white sands. This is where local women come to wash their clothes and then lay them out to dry in the sun.

The road leading up from the lake offers a panoramic view of the city in the distance with white sands and freshwater less than 1 km from the sea.

Beyond Itapoã are the magnificent ocean beaches of **Stella Maris** and **Flamengo**, both quiet during the week but very busy at the weekends. Beware of strong undercurrents in the sea.

The most well-known sight in the northern suburbs is the church of Nosso Senhor do Bonfim (Largo do Bomfim 236, Bonfim, T071-3316 2196, www.senhordobonfim. org.br, museum Tuesday-Friday 0800-1200 and 1400-1700, free; take bus S021-00 marked Ribeira-Pituba from the the *parada de ônibus* (bus stop) on Avenida da França on the quayside in the Cidade Baixa), (1745), on the Itapagipe Peninsula. It draws extraordinary numbers of supplicants (particularly on Friday and Sunday), making ex-voto offerings to the image of the Crucified Lord set over the high altar. The processions over the water to the church on the third Sunday in January are particularly interesting. The church has some naturalistic interior paintings by Franco Velasco (the modest canvases of the Stations of the Cross) and José Teófilo de Jesus (who painted the ceiling and 34 of the canvases on the church wall). Both almost certainly learnt their techniques from the master José Joaquim da Rocha.

The beach south of the church is far too dirty for swimming and is always busy with touts offering *fita* ribbons. It is the focus for celebrations during the festival of Nosso Senhor dos Navegantes. The colonial fort of **Monte Serrat** ⓘ *R Santa Rita Durão s/n, T071-3313 7339, Tue-Sun 0900-1700, US$0.50*, has unusual round towers. It is one of the best preserved colonial forts in northeast Brazil and was first constructed in 1583 and altered in the 18th and 19th centuries. It sits next to the pretty Portuguese church of **Nossa Senhora do Monte Serrat** on Monte Serrat – a much photographed local beauty spot overlooking the Baía de Todos os Santos and Bonfim beach.

Further north, at Ribeira, is the church of **Nossa Senhora da Penha** (1743), another beautiful colonial building and important syncretistic pilrgrimage site. The beach here has many restaurants, but is polluted.

## Listings Salvador *maps p28, p31, p36 and p39*

### Tourist information

**Bahiatursa**
*Av Simón Bolívar, 650, T071-3117 3000, www. bahiatursa.ba.gov.br. Mon-Fri 0830-1800.*
Salvador's main office, in Bahiatursa, has lists of hotels and accommodation in private homes, Staff can advise on travel throughout Bahia, and there are noticeboards for messages.

There are also branches at the following locations: **airport** (T071-3204 1244, daily 0730-2300); **Mercado Modelo** (Praça Visconde de Cayru 250, T071-3241 0242, Mon-Sat 0900-1800, Sun 0900-1330); **Pelourinho** (R das Laranjeiras 12, T071-3321 2133/2463, daily 0830-2100); **Rodoviária** (T071-3450 3871, daily 0730-2100); **Instituto Mauá**

(Praça Azevedo Fernandes 1, Porto da Barra, T071-3264 4671, Mon-Fri 0900-1800, Sat 1000-1500); **Shopping Barra** (Av Centenário, 2992, Chame-Chame, T071-3264 4566, Mon-Fri 0900-1900, Sat 0900-1400); and **Shopping Iguatemi** (Av Tancredo Neves 148, Pituba, T071-3480 5511, Mon-Fri 0900-2130, Sat 0900-1330).

### Where to stay

The Centro Histórico is the ideal place to stay. The Pelourinho is best if you're on a tight budget. Santo Antônio has reasonably priced hotels with charm and character. Barra also has some reasonable options; especially for apartments with kitchens, and it lies on the seafront. Business visitors will find good services and hotels in Rio Vermelho, overlooking the ocean and a 10-min taxi ride from the centre or airport.

Accommodation in the city tends to get very full over **Carnaval** and **New Year**, when prices go up. During **Carnaval** it is a good idea to rent a flat. The tourist office has a list of estate agents for flat rental (eg José Mendez, T071-3237 1394/6) or you can find flats through **Paradise Properties**, www.pp-bahia.com, **Bahia Online**, www.bahia-online.net, or **Bahia Land**, T071-8133 1441, williamwisden@gmail.com. Houses or rooms can be rented from **Pierre Marbacher**, R Carlos Coqueijo 68A, Itapoã, T071-3249 5754 (Caixa Postal 7458, 41600 Salvador), who is Swiss, owns a beach bar at Rua K and speaks English. Prices for the mid- and upper-end hotels are usually considerably cheaper when booked in advance through online travel agencies (OTAs) such as www. hotels.com and www.venere.com.

## The Pelourinho *map p36*

### $$$$ Casa do Amerelindo
*R das Portas do Carmo 6, T071-3266 8550, www.casado amarelindo.com.*
This refurbished colonial house offers a handful of well-appointed, modern a/c rooms, all with wooden floors and plain white walls decorated with local handicrafts. Those on the coastal side of the hotel have 2-m-tall shutter windows which open onto a sweeping view of the bay.

### $$$$ Hotel Villa Bahia
*Largo do Cruzeiro de São Francisco 16-18, T071-3322 4271, http://en.lavillabahia.com.*
This boutique hotel, part of the French **Voyeur** group, is housed in a renovated 18th-century townhouse right next to the the Convento de São Francisco. There's a little mosaic pool out back and a hot tub on the roof.

### $$$$ O Convento do Carmo
*R do Carmo 1, T071-3327 8400, www.pestana.com.*
Far and away the best in the city and the best historical hotel in the whole of Brazil, with a range of suites in a beautifully converted baroque convent. Facilities include an excellent restaurant and spa, a small swimming pool and business services.

### $$$ Bahia Café
*Praça Da Sé 22, T071-3322 1266, www.bahiacafehotel.com.*
*See Restaurants, below.*
This intimate little European-Brazilian boutique hotel is in a great location, 2 mins' walk from the Terreiro de Jesus and the Lacerda Lift. Rooms are rustic chic with chunky beds and brightly coloured counterpanes, but little furniture. Those at the front of the building sit over the street and can be noisy. Breakfasts are ample and there is an internet café serving great coffee on the ground floor.

### $$$ Hotel Pelourinho
*R Alfredo Brito 20, T071-3243 2324, www.hotelpelourinho.com.*
A refurbished 1960s hotel with bright tiled and white-walled a/c en suites. The bathrooms have marble basins and glass shower cubicles and a few offer great views out over the Baía de Todos os Santos.

### $$$ Studio do Carmo
*Ladeira do Carmo 17, T071-3326 2426, www.studiodocarmo.com.*
All rooms are large, decked out in wood and white paint and splashed with colour from bed linen and local art. The best are on the top floor and have terraces.

### $$$-$$ Solar das Artes
*R das Laranjeiras 34, T3481 0085, www.solardasartes.net.*
A lovely colonial house with a range of very simple wood-floor rooms (furnished with inelegant and ill-matched 1970s and 1980s fittings). The quietest are at the back. Some have very good views.

### $$ Albergue das Laranjeiras
*R Inácio Acciolli 13, T071-3321 1366, www.laranjeiras hostel.com.br.*

A big and brash HI hostel with a range of white-wall and tile-floor dorms and pricey doubles and triples in a colonial building in the heart of the historic centre. The breakfast area doubles up as a café and crêperie. English spoken and a full range of hostel services. The hostel can be noisy but is a good for meeting other travellers.

### Santo Antônio *map p31*

Santo Antônio is a quiet district just 5 mins' walk northeast of Pelourinho, beginning immediately after the Largo do Carmo. In recent years it has been a popular place for Europeans to open up carefully designed *pousadas* in beautifully restored buildings. A number have magnificent views of the bay. Most are mid-range, but there are a handful of cheaper options too.

### $$$$ Pousada Santo Antônio
*R Direita de Santo Antônio 130, T071-3326 1270, www.hotel-santoantonio.com.*
Stylish, bright and comfortable converted colonial townhouse, the best rooms have magnificent views out over the bay from your bed.

### $$$ Pousada do Boqueirão
*R Direita do Santo Antônio 48, T071-3241 2262, www.pousadaboqueirao.com.br.*
The most stylish of all the *pousadas* in Salvador. Lovingly renovated by the Italian interior designer owner and her brother, a former merchant seaman. There are a variety of themed rooms; the best at the top of the building, with wonderful views out over the Baía de Todos os Santos. Service and breakfast are excellent. Several languages spoken.

### $$$ Pousada do Pilar
*R Direita do Santo Antônio 24, T071-3241 6278, www.pousadadopilar.com.*
The a/c rooms are large, modern, decked out in raw wood and light plaster and have verandas with those excellent Baía de Todos os Santos views.

### $$$ Pousada Redfish
*Ladeira do Boqueirão 1, T071-3243 8473, www.hotelredfish.com.*
This English-owned stylish, lime-green boutique has plain, large rooms, some with terraces and open-air showers.

### $$$ Pousada Villa Carmo
*R do Carmo 58, T071-3241 3924, www.pousadavillacarmo.com.br.*
The simple but elegant a/c and fan-cooled rooms in this *pousadas* come with beautiful bay views. Look at several as some are a little cramped.

### $$ Hostel Nega Maluca
*R Dos Marchantes 15, Santo Antônio, T071-3242 9249, www.negamaluca.com.*
This popular party hostel is less than 400 m from one of Pelourinho's biggest Tue night shows. It has well-maintained but small rooms and dorms with thoughtful extras like a personal bed light and mains socket for each berth. The TV common room comes with complimentary hookahs, a cat and a dog and there's a terrace slung with hammocks.

### Porto da Barra and the Atlantic beach suburbs *map p39*

Barra is the most popular tourist neighbourhood close to the the historic centre and, whilst the sea is none too clean, the district has plenty of restaurants, beach bars and nightlife.

### $$$ Bahia Flat
*Av Oceânica 235, T071-3339 4140, www.bahiaflat.com.br.*
A range of flats, the best of which have sea views. Rooms are tastefully decorated and newly refurbished with Miró prints on the walls, patent leather sofas, glass coffee tables, large fridges, sound system and expansive mirror-fronted wardrobes. The hotel has a pool and sauna and internet.

### $$$ Monte Pascoal Praia
*Av Oceânica 176, Farol beach, T071-2103 4000, www.monte pascoalpraiahotel.com.br.*

A renovated 1970s hotel with simple rooms in tile and white paint, the best of which have views out over the bay.

## $$ Farol Barra Flat
*Av Oceanica 409, T071-3339 0000, www.farolbarraflat.com.br.*
More than 100 simple yet well-kept apartments with kitchenettes; all with microwaves, TVs and the best with sweeping ocean views. The best are the VIP suites – more spacious and on the top floors.

## $$ Pousada Hotel Âmbar
*R Afonso Celso 485, T071-3264 6956, www.ambarpousada.com.br.*
A French-owned *pousada* with very simple, small fan-cooled rooms gathered around a colourful little courtyard. The management practises ecotourism by contributing to the *criança familia* social project, recycling waste and conserving water.

## $$ Village Novo Beach suites
*Av 7 de Setembro 3659, T071-3267 4362, www.villagenovo.com.*
A 125-year-old converted townhouse with a range of tastefully decorated mock-boutique hotel rooms with terraces, a large roof patio and a pleasant little café restaurant. Look at several – some are far better than others. Many of those with a beach view are obscured by trees. The hotel has an internet café in the basement.

## $$ Villa Romana
*R Lemos Brito 14, T071-3264 6522, www.villaromana.com.br.*
Simple a/c rooms with wooden floors, desks, wardrobes and en suites and formal public areas decked out with mock 18th-century furnishings. There is a small patio with a pool behind the main building.

## $ Alpha Hostel
*R Eduardo Diniz Gonçalves 128, T071-3237 6282, www.alphahostel.com.*
The Salvador branch of this popular Rio hostel is tucked away on a small street a block from the beach and close to bus routes

on Av 7 de Setembro. Rooms and dorms are bright and colourful, but are fan-cooled only and can be stuffy – especially in the hotter months. Be wary along the backstreets in the area late at night.

## $ Hostel Che Lagarto Barra
*Av Oceânica 84B, T071-3235 2404, www.chelagarto.com.*
The Salvador branch of a busy South American party hostel chain sits in a big house less than 50 m from the beach and ideally positioned for the carnival parade. Dorms and doubles are spacious and bright, but they can be very noisy.

## $ La Villa Française
*R Recife 222, Jardim Brasil, T071-3245 6008, www.lavilafrancaise.com.*
A/c rooms are well tended, spruce and clean, and painted in bright lilacs, lemon yellows and eggshell blues. The helpful and knowledgeable French-Brazilian owners offer a sumptuous breakfast of pastries, fruit and cakes.

## $ Pousada Marcos
*Av Oceânica 281, T071-3264 5117, www.pousadamarcos.com.br.*
A very simple hostel-style guesthouse in a good location near the lighthouse. Always busy.

---

### Rio Vermelho *map p28*

## $$$$ Pestana Bahia
*R Fonte de Boi 216, T071-3453 8000, www.pestanahotels.com.br.*
A tower block with wonderful views out over the ocean but no access to the beach. Pool, gym, restaurant, sauna and very good business facilities. Online discounts available. With restaurant and bar.

## $$$$ Zank
*Av Almirante Barroso 161, Rio Vermelho, T071-3083 4000, www.zank hotel.com.br.*
This discreetly designed, expensive boutique hotel sits in a converted belle-époque house 5 mins' taxi ride from Rio Vermelho's bars and restaurants. Some rooms (notably No 10) have ocean views.

### $$$ Catharina Paraguaçu
*R João Gomes 128, Rio Vermelho, T071-3334 0089, www.hotelcatharinaparaguacu.com.br.*
Small colonial-style hotel with attractive courtyards and a range of decent rooms, some of which are distinctly better than others; look carefully and, if booking online, avoid the rooms close to the street. Very good service. Recommended.

### $$ Ibis
*R Fonte do Boi 215, T071-3330 8300, www.accorhotels.com.br.*
A vast, anonymous blocky hotel in this budget business chain, with functional rooms, some of which have sea views from the upper floors. Wi-Fi access throughout.

## Restaurants

**The Pelourinho** *map p36*

### $$$ Maria Mata Mouro
*R da Ordem Terceira 8, T071-3321 3929, www.mariamatamouro.com.br.*
International menu, excellent service, relaxing atmosphere in a quiet corner in the bustling Pelourinho.

### $$$ Sorriso de Dadá
*R Frei Vicente 5, T071-3321 9642.*
Bahia's most famous chef has cooked for, amongst others, Michael Palin, Jorge Amado, Gilberto Gil and Hillary Clinton. Her *moqueca de camarão* and her *vatapas* are signature dishes. When Dada is at the stove all is well, when she's not, the food is now very patchy and can be expensive.

### $$$ Uauá
*R Gregorio de Matos, 36, T071-3321 3089.*
Elegant, colonial restaurant and bar serving northeastern cooking and seafood, including some Bahian specialities. The restaurant's name means 'firefly' in Tupi.

### $$$-$$ Axego
*R João de Deus 1, T071-3242 7481.*
An established restaurant celebrated for its seafood. The *moquecas* are perhaps the best

in the Centro Histórico and there is excellent *feijoada* on Sun lunchtime. Meals are served in a pleasant upstairs dining room. In a great location less than a 1-min walk from the Terreiro de Jesus.

### $$$-$$ Jardim das Delícias
*R João de Deus, 12, T071-3321 1449.*
An award-winning, elegant restaurant and antiques shop set in a pretty tropical garden serving Bahian and international food accompanied by live classical or acoustic music. Very good value for its quality.

### $$ Mama Bahia
*R Portas do Carmo 21, T071-3322 4397, www.facebook.com/MamaBahia.*
Bahian and pan-Brazilian seafood served on white table cloths by waiters in bow ties and suits. Popular dishes include *camarão tropical* (cooked in pineapple skin and served *gratinada* in a tangy sauce). Live acoustic music most nights.

### $$ Mão Dupla
*R Santa Isabel 10, T071-9916 0217.*
On a quiet side street off bustling R das Laranjeiras. Chef Sandra serves great-value traditional northeastern and Bahian dishes from *bobó do camarão* to myriad *moquecas* in portions big enough for 2. Veggie options also available. Nice atmosphere.

### $$ Senac
*Praça José Alencar 13-15, Largo do Pelourinho, T071-3324 4557.*
A catering school with 2 restaurants. Upstairs is typical Bahian cooking; downstairs is per kilo and open only for lunch; both are a/c. Dishes are better upstairs but there is plenty of choice in the buffet and options for vegetarians.

### $ Bahia Café
*Praça da Sé 20, T071-3322 1266.*
Smart, Belgian-run internet café with good coffee, a European-style breakfast menu and decent snacks. Located in the **Bahia Café** hotel (see Where to stay, above).

## Bahian cuisine

Bahian cooking is spiced and peppery. The main dish is *moqueca* – seafood cooked in a sauce made from coconut milk, tomatoes, red and green peppers, fresh coriander and *dendê* (palm oil). It is traditionally cooked in a wok-like earthenware dish and served piping hot at the table. *Moqueca* is often accompanied by *farofa* (manioc flour) and a hot pepper sauce which you add at your discretion; it's very mild by British or Asian standards. The *dendê* is somewhat heavy and those with delicate stomachs are advised to try the *ensopado*, a sauce with the same ingredients as the *moqueca*, but without the palm oil.

Nearly every street corner has a Bahiana selling a wide variety of local snacks, the most famous of which is the *acarajé*, a kidney bean dumpling fried in palm oil, which has its origins in West Africa. To this the *Bahiana* adds *vatapá*, a dried shrimp and coconut milk paté (also delicious on its own), *pimenta* (hot sauce) and fresh salad. For those who prefer not to eat the palm oil, the *abará* is a good substitute. *Abará* is steamed and wrapped in banana leaves.

Bahians usually eat *acarajé* or *abará* with a chilled beer on the way home from work or the beach at sunset. Another popular dish with African origins is *xin-xin de galinha*, chicken on the bone cooked in *dendê*, with dried shrimp, garlic and squash.

### $ Café Gourmet
*R da Bispo 5, Praça da Sé, no telephone.*
Cuban-style café serving sandwiches. Excellent coffee and tea served in china cups. Doubles as a cigar shop.

### $ Gramado
*Praça da Sé 16/18, T071-3494 3502. Lunch only.*
The best of the few per kilo restaurants in the area. Scrupulously clean and with a reasonable choice.

### South of the centre *map p31*

### $$$ Amado
*Av Lafayete Coutinho 660, Comércio, T071-3322 3520, www.amadobahia.com.br.*
The best of Salvador's top-end restaurants on the Baía de Todos os Santos waterfront. The space is beautiful, set on a deck overlooking the lapping aquamarine of the Baía de Todos os Santos. The haute cuisine *moquecas* are excellent.

### $$$ SoHo
*Av Contorno 1010, Bahia Marina, T071-3322 4554, http://sohorestaurante.com.br/en.*
The restaurant's long bar is where Salvador's 'A-list' drink their caipirinhas. Great sushi and sashimi combinations from Paulistano chef Marcio Fushimi are served in the chic glass-walled dining room and at the open-air veranda tables overlooking the ocean.

### Porto da Barra and the Atlantic beach suburbs *map p39*
There are many a/c restaurants from cheap to medium-priced in **Shopping Barra** and the **Barra Center Shopping**.

### $$$ Barravento
*Av Oceanica 814, T071-3247 2577, www.restaurantebarravento.com.br.*
Very popular beach bar restaurant and hang-out with a marquee roof. Decent cocktails, *chope* and a menu of seafood, *moquecas* and steaks.

### $$ Quatro Amicci
*R Dom Marcos Teixeira 35, T071-3264 3333.*
Excellent wood-fired oven pizzas served in a bright modern space in a converted 19th-century house. Lively weekend crowd.

## $ Caranguejo do Farol
*Av Oceânica 235, T071-3264 7061.*
A buzzing bar and seafood restaurant serving great Bahian food in *refeição* portions large enough for 2. Cheap bottled beer. Strong caipirinhas.

## Rio Vermelho and other neighbourhoods *map p28*

### $$$ Paraiso Tropical
*R Edgar Loureiro, 98-B, Resgate, Cabula, T071-3384 7464, www.restauranteparaiso tropical.com.br.*
It's a long taxi ride from Barra or the historical centre, but there is no better Bahian restaurant in Salvador. Beto Pimentel's inventive Bahian cooking has earned him accolades from the Commanderie Des Cordons Bleus De France and *Veja* magazine's restaurant critics. Dishes are contemporary takes on Bahian and northeastern Brazilian cooking, made with organic ingredients grown in the kitchen garden. And Beto himself is a colourful character with an equally colourful life story.

### $$ Casa da Dinha
*R João Gomes 25, Rio Vermelho, just west of the Catharina Paraguaçu Hotel and a few yards from the Largo de Santana, T071-3334 4350.*
One of the best mid-range Bahian restaurants in the city with a varied menu peppered with Bahian specialities, steaks, fish and standard international options like pasta.

### $$ Restaurante Oceânico
*R Pedra da Sereia 66, Rio Vermelho, T071-9350 1555, www.facebook.com/ RestauranteOceanico. Open until late, especially on weekends.*
A long-established popular Bahian seafood restaurant.

## Bars and clubs

Nightlife is concentrated on and around the Pelourinho and the Terreiro de Jesus, where there is always a free live street band on Tue and at weekends. The Pelourinho area is also a good place to browse the bars, but be wary after 2300. There are many bars on the Largo de Quincas Berro d'Água, and along R Alfredo do Brito. R João de Deus and its environs are dotted with simple pavement bars with plastic tables.

The most famous music from Salvador is the *batucada* of drum orchestras like **Olodum** and **Ilê Aiyê**, whose impressive sound can be heard frequently around the Pelourinho (Olodum played on Paul Simon's *Rhythm of the Saints* album). Both groups have their own venues and play in the individual parades or *blocos* at Carnaval.

### Cantina da Lua
*Praça Quinze de Novembro 2, Terreiro de Jesus, T071-3322 4041. Daily.*
Popular spot on the square with outdoor seating, but gets crowded and the food isn't great.

### Casa do Olodum
*R Gregório de Matos 22, T071-3321 4154, www.olodum.com.br.*
Olodum's headquarters where they perform live every Tue and Sun at 1900 to packed crowds.

### Loja do Ilê Aiyê
*R das Laranjeiras 16, T071-3321 4193, www.ileaiyeoficial.com.*
Ilê Aiyê's headquarters and shop, where you can find information about their shows and **Carnaval** events.

### O Cravinho
*Praça 15 de Novembro 3, T071-3322 6759, www.ocravinho.com.br.*
Dark little bar with occasional live music. Always busy. Greasy bar food is served at tree-trunk tables, usually accompanied by plentiful *cachaça*, which is made here and stored in barrels behind the bar. Be careful in this area after 2300.

## Porto da Barra and the Atlantic beach suburbs *map p39*
Barra nightlife is concentrated around the **Farol da Barra** (lighthouse) and **R Marquês**

## ON THE ROAD
### Bahia's musicians recommend

Mariene de Castro is one of Brazil's most exciting samba acts. Her debut CD *Abre Caminho* won several of Brazil's top music awards in 2007 and she is well known in Brazil for reinvigorating and re-inventing traditional North Eastern Brazilian music styles.

She told *Footprint* where to go out in Salvador: "The best and most exciting music in Bahia has its roots firmly in the samba tradition. Some of the best artists are members of the Santo de Casa cultural movement who play in the Praça Pedro Arcanjo near the Pelourinho and the Espaço Cultural Barroquinha, Praça da Barroquinha (1 km south of the Pelourinho), T061-3334 7350, Facebook: ecbarroquinha."

Carlinhos Brown is one of Brazil's greatest percussionists and the founder of the Timbalada drum troupe. He is one of the icons of Bahian music and a star of Carnaval. We asked him where to go to hear live music in Salvador: "At our community centre here in Candeal you can hear my band Timbalada as well as great acts like Candombless and Beat Gabot and in the African music centre." The African music centre is the Museu do Ritmo (T071-3242 0214, Facebook: Museu-Du-Ritmo). Find out when Carlinhos Brown's concerts are during your visit on his website, www.carlinhosbrown.com.br. More recent acts on the scene include Metá Metá, who fuse Bahian rhythms with afro-beat, and singer Juliana Ribeiro.

de Leão, which is busy with pavement bars. Like the Pelourinho the whole area is good for a browse, but be wary of pickpockets.

### Rio Vermelho *map p28*
The district of Rio Vermelho was once the bohemian section of town and it still has good live music and exciting bar nightlife. There are a number of lively bars around the Largo de Santana, a block west of **Hotel Catharina Paraguaçu**. The *bairro* as a whole is well worth exploring on a bar crawl Thu-Sun.

### Casa da Mãe
*R Guedes Cabral 81, T071-3037-9663, www. facebook.com/espacoculturalcasadamae.* Live *samba de roda* several times a week and roots Bahian music. Ring ahead for schedule.

### Entertainment

The **Fundação Cultural do Estado da Bahia** edits *Bahia Cultural*, a monthly brochure listing the main cultural events for the month. These can be found in most

hotels and **Bahiatursa** information centres. Local newspapers *A Tarde* and *Correio da Bahia* have good listing for cultural events in the city.

### Cinema
The main shopping malls show mainstream Hollywood and international films, almost invariably dubbed (*dublado*). Only a few showings have subtitles (*legendas*).

### Live music
**Concha Acústica**, *Teatro Castro Alves, Praça 2 de Julho, Campo Grande, T071-3339 8000, www.tca.ba.gov.br.* The city's premier small concert venue with quality national and international acts such as Tom Zé and Naná Vasconcelos.

**Teatro Sesi Rio Vermelho**, *R Borges dos Reis 9, T071-3616 7064, www.portalsesicriativo. com.br.* One of the best venues in the city for contemporary Bahian bands.

**Theatro Castro** Alves, *Largo 2 de Julho, Campo Grande, T071-3339 8000.* The city's most distinguished performance space

## Why I love carnival in Bahia

"I love that Carnival in Salvador is so huge (some 3 million people) and so diverse. We have the popular fun of *axé* music, samba and other styles, alongside Brazil's African heritage, with the *afoxés* – some of which were founded in the first half of the 20th century – and the Afro *blocos*. Don't miss the parade by our oldest Afro *bloco*, Ilê Aiyê (35 years old), which mixes this heritage with exuberant joy and religious reverence".

*Tiganá Santana, Bahia's foremost contemporary singer-songwriter whose CDs include 2015's spellbinding* Tempo & Magma.

and the home of the Bahian Symphony Orchestra and the Castro Alves Ballet Company. The theatre also hosts occasional performances by more cerebral MPB artists and contemporary performers like Hermeto Pascoal or Egberto Gismonti.

### Festivals

**6 Jan Epiphany**. Public holiday with many free concerts and events. Beautiful Masses in many of the historic churches.

**Jan Festa do Nosso Senhor do Bonfim**. Held on the 2nd Sun after Epiphany. On the preceding Thu there is a colourful parade at the church with many penitents and a ceremonial washing of the church itself. Great for photographs.

**Feb Carnaval**, see box, page 52.

**2 Feb Pescadores do Rio Vermelho**. Boat processions with gifts for Yemanjá, Goddess of the Sea, accompanied by African Brazilian music.

**Mar/Apr Holy Week**. The week before Easter sees many colourful processions around the old churches in the upper city.

### Shopping

#### Arts, crafts and cigars

**Artesanato Santa Bárbara**, *R Alfredo Brito 7, Pelourinho, T071-3321 2685*. Excellent handmade lace.

**Atelier Totonho and Raimundo**, *Ladeira do Carmo, Pelourinho*. 2 adjacent galleries run by a co-operative of some 28 naïve art artists,

including Totonho, Calixto, Raimundo Santos and Jô. Good prices.

**FIEB-SESI**, *Av Tiradentes 299, Bonfim; Av Borges dos Reis 9, Rio Vermelho; and Av 7 de Setembro 261, Mercês*. Some of the best artisan products in the city ranging from textiles and ceramics to musical instruments.

**Goya Lopes**, *R Gregorio de Mattos, Pelourinho, T071-3321 9428, www.goyalopes.com.br*. African-Brazilian designer clothing on Goya's Didara label, which features very simple, rustic cotton clothing and beach shawls stamped with intricate motifs in very bright colours from Afro-Brazilian cultural life.

**Instituto Mauá**, *R Gregorio de Matos 27, Pelourinho. Tue-Sat 0900-1800, Sun 1000-1600*. Good-quality items, better value and quality than the Mercado Modelo.

**Loja de Artesanato do SESC**, *Largo Pelourinho, T071-3321 5502. Mon-Fri 0900-1800 (closed for lunch), Sat 0900-1300*.

**Oficina de Investigação Musical**, *Alfredo Brito 24, Pelourinho, T071-3322 2386, www.facebook.com/oficinadeinvstigacaomusical. Mon-Fri 0800-1200 and 1300-1600*. Handmade traditional percussion instruments (and percussion lessons for US$9 per hr).

**Rosa do Prado**, *R Inacio Aciolly 5, Pelourinho*. Cigar shop packed with every kind of Brazilian *charuto* imaginable.

#### Bookshops

**Graúna**, *Av 7 de Setembro 1448, and R Barão de Itapoã 175, Porto da Barra*. English titles.

**Sebo Brandão**, *R Ruy Barbosa 4, Centre, T071-3243 5383*. Second-hand English, French, Spanish and German books.

## Jewellery
**Casa Moreira**, *Ladeira da Praça, just south of Praça da Sé*. Exquisite jewellery and antiques. Most are expensive, but there are some affordable charms.
**Scala**, *Praça da Sé, T071-3321 8891*. Handmade jewellery using locally mined gems (eg aquamarine, amethyst and emerald), workshop at back.

## Markets
**Feira de Artesanato**, *Santa Maria Fort. Wed 1700-2100*. Arts and crafts in the fort at the far end of Porto da Barra beach.
**Feira de São Joaquim**, *5 km from Mercado Modelo along the seafront. Daily 0800-1900, Sun 0800-1200*. The largest and least touristy market in the city selling mainly foodstuffs and a few artisan products. Very smelly.
**Mercado Modelo**, *Praça Cairu, Cidade Baixa. Sat 0800-1900, Sun 0800-1200*. Live music and dancing, especially Sat. Expect to be asked for money if you take photos. Many tourist items such as woodcarvings, silver-plated fruit, leather goods, local musical instruments. Lace items for sale are often not handmade (despite labels), are heavily marked up, and are much better bought at their place of origin (eg Ilha de Maré, Pontal da Barra and Marechal Deodoro).

## Music and carnival souvenirs
**Boutique Olodum**, *Praça José Alencar, Pelourinho*. Olodum CDs, music, T-shirts and musical instruments.
**Cana Brava Records**, *R João de Deus 22, T071-3321 0536, www.bahia-online.net*. Great little CD shop with a friendly and knowledgeable American owner. Stocks a whole range of classy Brazilian artists, less internationally famous names and back catalogue artists.
**Ilê Aiyê**, *R das Laranjeiras 16, T071-3321 4193, www.ileaiye.org.br*. Bags, clothes, books,

music and other such items from this famous Carnaval drum orchestra and *bloco*.

## Shopping centres
These are the most comfortable places to shop in Salvador – havens of a/c cool in the heat of the Bahian summer offering a chance to rest over an ice-cold beer, to lunch and to shop for essentials like Havaianas, bikinis, CDs and beach wraps along with comestibles like batteries, supermarket food and sunscreen.
**Shopping Barra**, *Av Centenário 2992, Chame-Chame, Barra, T071-2108 8288, www.shopping barra.com*. The largest shopping mall within easy access of the tourist centres.
**Shopping Iguatemi**, *Av Tancredo Neves 148, Caminho das Árvores, T071-2126 1111, www.iguatemisalvador.com.br*. Next to the *rodoviária*, with a broad spread of mid- to upmarket shops, a large a/c food court and cinemas on the top floor.
**Salvador Shopping**, *Av Tancredo Neves 3133, Caminho das Árvores, www.salvadorshopping. com.br*. One of the city's largest, plushest and newest with an excellent cinema and the best selection of upper-end brands.

## What to do

### Capoeira
There are many capoeira schools offering classes in and around the Pelourinho.
**Associação de Capoeira Mestre Bimba**, *R das Laranjeiras 1, Pelourinho, T071-3322 0639, www.capoeiramestrebimba.com.br*. This school is the inheritor of the teaching of Mestre Bimba, who was the first master to define a system for teaching capoeira regional. There are both male and female teachers.
**Escola de Capoeira Angola Irmãos Gêmeos**, *R Gregório de Mattos 9, Pelourinho, T071-3321 0396/9963 3562, http://ecaig. blogspot.com (also on Facebook)*. A school founded by Mestre Curió, who learnt with another legendary capoeirista, Mestre Pastinha. Classes are broad and are good for women, children and older people. In

# FESTIVALS

## Carnaval in Bahia

Carnival in Bahia is the largest in the world and encourages active participation. It is said that there are 1.5 million people dancing on the streets at any one time.

The **pre-carnival festive season** begins with São Nicodemo de Cachimbo (penultimate Sunday of November), followed by Santa Bárbara (4 December), then the Festa da Conceição da Praia, centred on the church of that name (open 0700-1130) at the base of the Lacerda lift. The last night is 8 December (not for those who don t like crowds!). The Festa da Boa Viagem takes place in the last week of December, in the lower city; the beach will be packed all night on 31 December. The new year kicks off on 1 January with a beautiful boat procession of Nosso Senhor dos Navegantes from Conceição da Praia to the church of Boa Viagem, on the beach of that name in the lower city. The leading boat, which carries the image of Christ and the archbishop, was built in 1892. You can follow in a sailing boat for about US$1; go early (0900) to the dock by the Mercado Modelo. A later festival is São Lázaro on the last Sunday in January.

Carnaval itself officially starts on Thursday night at 2000 when the keys of the city are given to the Carnaval King '*Rei Momo*'. The unofficial opening though is on Wednesday with the Lavagem do Porto da Barra, when throngs of people dance on the beach. Later in the evening is the Baile dos Atrizes, starting at around 2300 and going on until dawn, very bohemian, good fun. Check with **Bahiatursa** for details on venue and time (also see box, page 11, for Carnaval dates).

There are two distinct musical formats. The **afro blocos** are large drum-based troupes (some with up to 200 drummers) who play on the streets, accompanied by singers atop mobile sound trucks. The first of these groups was the Filhos de Gandhy (founded in 1949), whose participation is one of the highlights of Carnaval. Their 6000 members dance through the streets on the Sunday and Tuesday of Carnaval dressed in their traditional costumes, a river of white and blue in an ocean of multi-coloured carnival revellers. The best known of the recent *afro blocos* are Ilê Aiye, Olodum, Muzenza and Malê Debalê. They all operate throughout the year in cultural, social and political areas. Not all of them are receptive to foreigners among their numbers for Carnaval. The basis of the rhythm is the enormous *surdo* (deaf) drum with its *bumbum bumbum bum* anchorbeat, while the smaller repique, played with light twigs, provides a crack-like overlay. Ilê Aiye take to the streets around 2100 on Saturday night and their departure from their headquarters at Ladeira do Curuzu in the Liberdade district is not to be missed. The best way to get there is to take a taxi to Curuzu via Largo do Tanque,

Curió's absence classes are conducted by the mestre's pupil, Mestra Jararaca (the first woman to earn the Mestra tiltle in Capoeira Angola).
**Forte de Santo Antônio Alem do Carmo**, *T071-3117 1488*. Has a number of schools teaching capoeira, usually in the evenings.

They include **Pele da Bahia** (T071-3387 6485), and **Mestre Boca Rica** (T071-3401 3019).
**Grupo Cultural de Capoeira Angola Moçambique**, *R Gregório de Mattos 38, Pelourinho, T071-8113 7455*. Offers tuition in Capoeira Angola. Teaching is very flexible, with options for either day classes or full terms and it also offers berimbau and

thereby avoiding traffic jams. The ride is a little longer but much quicker. A good landmark is the Paes Mendonça supermarket on the corner of the street, from where the *bloco* leaves. From there it s a short walk to the departure point.

The enormous **trios eléctricos**, 12-m sound trucks with powerful sound systems that defy most decibel counters, are the second format. These trucks, each with its town band of up to 10 musicians, play songs influenced by the *afro blocos* and move at a snail's pace through the streets, drawing huge crowds. Each *afro bloco* and *bloco de trio* has its own costume and its own security personnel, who cordon off the area around the sound truck. The *bloco* members can thus dance in comfort and safety.

The traditional Carnaval route is from Campo Grande (by the Tropical Hotel da Bahia) to Praça Castro Alves near the old town. The *blocos* go along Avenida 7 de Setembro and return to Campo Grande via the parallel Rua Carlos Gomes. Many of the trios no longer go through the Praça Castro Alves, once the epicentre of Carnaval. The best night at Praça Castro Alves is Tuesday (the last night of Carnaval), when the famous *Encontro dos Trios'* (Meeting of the Trios) takes place. *Trios* jostle for position in the square and play in rotation until the dawn on Ash Wednesday. It is not uncommon for major stars from the Bahian (and Brazilian) music world to make surprise appearances.

There are grandstand seats at Campo Grande throughout the event. Day tickets for these are available the week leading up to Carnaval. Check with Bahiatursa for information on where the tickets are sold. The *blocos* are judged as they pass the grandstand and are at their most frenetic at this point. There is little or no shade from the sun so bring a hat and lots of water. Best days are Sunday to Tuesday. For those wishing to go it alone, just find a friendly *barraca* in the shade and watch the *blocos* go by. Avoid the Largo da Piedade and Relógio de São Pedro on Avenida 7 de Setembro: the street narrows here, creating human traffic jams.

The other major centre for Carnaval is Barra to Ondina. The **blocos alternativos** ply this route. These are nearly always *trios eléctricos*, connected with the more traditional *blocos* who have expanded to this now very popular district. Not to be missed here is Timbalada, the drumming group formed by the internationally renowned percussionist Carlinhos Brown.

Ticket prices in the grandstands (*camarotes*) cost between US$200 and US$450. Tickets in cordoned-off dance areas within the *blocos* themselves within the street parades (known as *abadas*, and coming with a unique identifying T-shirt) cost from US$50-US$400 depending on the *bloco* you are joining.

The quality of the *bloco* often depends on the act that plays on the *trio*. For more information see the official Carnaval site, www.carnaval. salvador.ba.gov.br.

percussion lessons. Famous teachers include mestres Boca Rica and Neco – alumni of Canjiquinha and Waldemar – 2 of the most celebrated teachers of the 20th century.

#### Football
**Itaipava Arena Fonte Nova**, *Ladeira da Fonte das Pedras, Nazaré, T071-3320 2161, www.* *itaipavaarenafontenova.com.br.* 55,000-seat stadium used for the 2014 FIFA World Cup™, which is home to the **Esporte Clube Bahia** and **Vitória** football clubs. 10 mins away from the Pelourinho, and the Barroquinha terminal and fully rebuilt for 2014. It will be a football venue in the 2016 Olympics.

## Language courses

Salvador is a popular place to learn Portuguese. In addition to the places listed below, classes can be organized through www.portugueseinbrazil.com and www.dialogo-brazilstudy.com.

**Casa do Brasil**, *R Milton de Oliveira 231, Barra, T071-3264 5866, www.casadobrazil.com.br.* Portuguese for foreigners.

**Diálogo**, *R Dr João Pondé 240, Barra, T071-3264 0007, www.dialogo-brazilstudy.com.* With optional dance, *capoeira* and cooking classes and accommodation arranged with host families.

**Superlearning Idiomas**, *Av 7 de Setembro 3402, Ladeira da Barra, T071-3337 2824, www.allways.com.br/spl.*

## Music and percussion

**Diaspora**, *R da Laranjeiras 44, T071-9998 8488.* Afternoon and evening *afoxe*, samba and *axê* dance, percussion music classes and other courses on African Bahia (including candomble). Classes from US$3 depending on numbers (minimum 2 people) when bought in a block of several classes.

**Escola do Olodum**, *R das Laranjeiras 30, T071-3322 8069.* Classes from the masters of the Olodum school itself. Minimum 10 people, US$40 per hr per person.

## Tour operators

Bus tours are available from several companies, including: the **Salvador Bus** (see below); **Alameda Turismo** (*R Fernando Menezes de Góes 397, Pituba, T071-2107 5999, US$25 per person*); and **Tours Bahia** (*Largo do Cruzeiro de São Francisco 4/6, Centro Histórico, T071-3320 3280, www.toursbahia.com.br*).

**Cultour**, *R João Gomes, 88 Sala 8 Sobrado da Praça, Rio Vermelho, T071-3335 1062, www.cultour.it.* Offers some of the best cultural tours in the city. Less 'touristy' than operators in the Pelourinho area.

**Ilha Bela**, *Av da França, T071-3326 7158, www.ilhabelatm.com.br.* Tours around the Baía de Todos os Santos and transfers to Morro de São Paulo.

**Salvador Bus**, *T071-3356 6425, www.salvadorbus.com.br.* Runs coach tours of the city with a commentary in Portuguese and English. Buses are a/c on the lower deck and open-topped above (with a covering for when it rains) and call at Rio Vermelho, Orla Marítima (esplanade), Farol da Barra lighthouse and beach, the forts, Museu de Arte da Bahia, Praça Castro Alves, the Pelourinho, Elevador Lacerda, Igreja do Bonfim, Solar de Unhão and Museu de Arte Moderna, and Dique do Tororó. They are hop-on/hop-off with a wristband ticket (US$13.50, US$9.80 for children aged 3-12). 5 buses a day are scheduled (currently 0830-1900) though in reality the service is sporadic and unpredictable. Tickets can be bought at travel agencies, hotels, commercial centres, **Iguatemi Shopping** (Salvador) and on the buses themselves.

**Tatur Turismo**, *Av Tancredo Neves 274, Centro Empresarial Iguatemi, Salas 222-224, T071-3114 7900, www.tatur.com.br.* Excellent private tours of the city and the state as well as general travel agency services including flight booking and accommodation. Can organize entire packages prior to arrival for the whole of Brazil. Good English, reliable. Irish-owned.

## Transport

### Air

To get to the airport: a/c *combis* leave from Praça da Sé bus stop via the coast road and Barra 0630-2100, US$4, 1-1½ hrs (1 hr from Barra). Ordinary buses marked 'Aeroporto' run from the same stop and cost US$0.85. A taxi to the airport costs around US$20 (US$25-40 after 2200 and on weekends and public holidays). Travel agencies and some hotels can also organize transfers.

There are domestic flights to all of Brazil's major cities, some with connections through **Recife**, **Belo Horizonte** or **São Paulo**; the best prices are usually to **Rio de Janeiro** and

**São Paulo**. There are international flights to **Madrid** (3 times weekly with **Air Europa**), **Frankfurt** (once weekly with **Condor**), **Lisbon** (daily with **TAP**), **Milan** (once weekly with **Air Italy**) and weekly flights to **Miami** in the USA with **American Airlines**.

Airlines flying from Salvador include: **Addey**, **Avianca**, **Azul**, **Gol** and **TAM**. International flights are with **Air Europa**, **Condor** and **TAP**.

## Bus

**Local**  Standard buses cost US$0.85 single; a/c *executivos* cost US$1.25-2 depending on the route. On buses and at the ticket sellers' booths, watch your change and beware of pickpockets (one scam used by thieves is to descend from the bus while you are climbing aboard). For details on buses in Salvador visit www.meubuzu.com.br (in Portuguese but easy to follow).

Buses are fast and frequent. The main bus stop in the Centro Histórico is at the southern end of Praça Municipal (Tomé de Sousa). Buses marked 'Barra' and 'Campo Grande-Praça da Sé' run between the **Praça da Sé** in the Centro Histórico and **Barra**. There are a number of lines including M024-00 and M024-01 (both via R Carlos Gomes, Av 7 de Setembro and Praça 2 Julho in Campo Grande). To get between the **airport** and Centro Histórico, Barra and the beaches, catch the S002-00 'Aeroporto-Praça da Sé' bus, which leaves from the **Praça da Se**, passing Av 7 de Setembro (Centre), Av 7 de Setembro and Av Oceânica in **Barra**, Av Oceânica in **Ondina**, R Paciencia, R João Gomes and R Osvaldo Cruz in **Rio Vermelho**, continuing on through **Amaralina**, **Pituba** and **Itapoã**, before turning in to the airport (1st bus 0500, last bus 2210). The 1002-00 'Aeroporto-Campo Grande' bus follows a similar route beginning at Av 7 de Setembro in the centre (1st bus 0545, last bus 2300). The most comfortable and quickest of these buses are the a/c *frescão*.

For the ocean beaches, take buses S011-00, S011-01 and S011-02 marked 'Praça da Sé-Flamengo'. These run to **Flamengo Beach** (30 km from the city), following the coastal route, passing through **Campo Grande** and **Barra** and all the best beaches (including **Stella Maris** and **Itapoã**), and leaving from Praça da Sé, US$3.50; sit on the right-hand side for the best views (1st 0600, last 1930). For **Bonfim** and **Ribeira**, take one of the following: bus S021-00 marked 'Ribeira-Pituba' calls at Ribeira, R Imperatriz, next to the Igreja do Bonfim, Av da Franca 200 m north of the Mercado Modelo, Av Juracy Magalhaes Jr in Rio Vermelho and Pituba Beach; 'Bus S027-00' marked 'Ribeira Campo Grande' calls at Ribeira, the Ladeira do Bonfim near the church, R Itapicuru at R Jacuipe in Mont Serrat, Av da Franca 200 m north of the Mercado Modelo, R Carlos Gomes and the Av 7 Setembro in the centre and in Campo Grande (near the Mosteiro São Bento) and Av Setembro in Barra. Bus 0219-00 runs between Ribeira and the *rodoviária*, leaving from R Travas Fora in Bonfim.

**Long-distance**  To get to the *rodoviária* take bus RI or RII, 'Centro-Rodoviária-Circular' (US$1), from the Lower City at the foot of the Lacerda Lift; the journey can take up to 1 hr, especially at peak periods. On weekdays, a quicker executive bus (US$1.25) runs from Praça da Sé or Praça da Inglaterra (by McDonalds), Comércio, to **Iguatemi Shopping Centre** from where there is a walkway to the *rodoviária* (take care in the dark). Alternatively, take a bus from the centre, US$9.

There are frequent services to the majority of destinations; a large panel in the main hall of the bus terminal lists destinations and the relevant ticket office. For bus information contact the *rodoviária*, Av Antônio Carlos Magalhães 4362, T071-3460 8300, daily 0600-2200, and see www.aguiabranca.com.br, www.realexpresso.com.br and www.gontijo.com.br.

To **Aracaju**, 3 daily (1st 0630, last 2200), 4½ hrs, US$18, *leito* US$25 with Bomfim. To **Belém**, US$85 *comercial* with Itapemirim.

To **Ilhéus**, 8 daily, 7 hrs, US$25, *executivo* US$35, *leito* US$80 with **Bomfim**. To **Maceio**, 4 daily, 1st at 0630, last 2200, 4½ hrs, US$30, *leito* US$67 with **Bomfim**. To **Porto Seguro**, 1 daily at 2000, 10 hrs, US$50 with **Aguia Branca**. To **Recife**, US$45, 13 hrs, 1 daily and 1 *leito*, with **Itapemerim**, T071-3358 0037. To **Rio de Janeiro**, Mon-Sat 0700, 26 hrs, US$85, *leito* US$95, with **Itapemirim** and **Aguia Branca**; good stops, clean toilets, recommended. To **São Paulo**, 30 hrs, US$80, US$95, with **São Geraldo** (Mon, Wed and Fri at 0830 and 1930, Sun, Mon and Sat at 2000), daily *leito* at 2200. To **Fortaleza**, 20 hrs, US$65 at 0900 with **Itapemirim**. To **Lençóis** at 2200, 6-8 hrs, US$20 with **Real Expresso**, via Feira de Santana, T071-3358 1591. To **Belo Horizonte**, Gontijo, T071-3358 7448, at 1700, US$80. There are also bus services to **Brasília** along the fully paved BR-242, via **Barreiras**, 3 daily, 23 hrs; **Palmas**, **Natal**, **João Pessoa**, **Penedo** (via **Maceio**), **Vitória** and **Teresina**. For the shortest route to **Valença**, take the ferry from São Joaquim to Bom Despacho on Itaparica island, from where it is 130 km to Valença via **Nazaré das Farinhas** (see page 58).

## Car hire

There are various car hire booths in the airport: **Hertz**, www.hertz.com.br, **Interlocadora**, www.interlocadora.com.br, and **Localiza**, www.localiza.com.

## Taxi

Meters start at US$0.85 and then US$0.50 per 100 m. They charge US$15 per hr within city limits, and 'agreed' rates outside. **Taxi Barra-Centro**, US$7 daytime; US$9 at night. Watch the meter; the night time charge should be 30% higher than daytime charges. **Teletaxi** (24-hr service), T071-3321 9988.

## Ferry and boat

See also Ilha de Itaparica, page 58. Boats and catamarans to **Ilha de Itaparica** and other islands in the Baía de Todos os leave from the main ferry dock, **Marítimo de São Joaquim**, Av Oscar Pontes 1051, T071-3254 1020, www.agerba.ba.gov.br/transporteHidroviario Ferry.htm. There are 10 car ferries per day to Itaparica. Passenger boats for Itaparica and **Morro de São Paulo** (2½ hrs) leave from Salvador's other boat terminal, the **Terminal Marítimo de Mercado Modelo** (or Terminal Marítimo Turistico). See www.morrodesaopaulocatamara.com for the latest ferry timetables.

# Around
## Salvador

The Baía de Todos os Santos is Brazil's largest bay and is dotted with islands; many of them are privately owned, others serving as weekend resorts for people from Salvador. The best known is Itaparica, a long, thin island lined with palms, with a pretty colonial capital and some reasonable beaches. Many buses run from here, and taking the ferry across from Salvador and then road transport from Itaparica is the quickest way to get to southern Bahia.

The area around the bay and immediately west of Salvador (on the other side of the Baía de Todos os Santos) is known as the Recôncavo Baiano. This fertile hinterland is where agriculture in Brazil was born, and where hundreds of thousands of indigenous Brazilians and enslaved Africans sweated and died to harvest sugar cane, cocoa and coffee.

It is dotted with sleepy colonial towns with some fine architecture. The most famous places are Cachoeira and its twin settlement São Felix, on the banks of the muddy Rio Paraguaçu. They are famous for their festivals and strong connection to *candomblé*. There are also small fishing villages on the bay that are worth exploring, and dotted throughout the countryside are the decaying ruins of once-productive *engenhos* (sugar refineries), some of which can be visited.

Salvador sits on a peninsula which forms the northern head of Brazil's largest bay, the Baía de Todos os Santos. The bay is studded with tropical islands, the largest of which, Itaparica, sits immediately opposite Salvador, forming the bay's southern head. Itaparica is the only island close to Salvador with water clean enough for swimming. It is only 29 km long and 12 km wide and can easily be visited on a day trip.

There are two tiny towns on the island and a cluster of hamlets. **Itaparica** is very picturesque and well worth a visit, with a decent beach and many fine residential buildings from the 19th century. The church of **São Lourenço** is one of the oldest in Brazil, and a stroll through the old town is delightful. In summer the streets are ablaze with the blossoms of the beautiful flamboyant trees.

Itaparica town is connected to the main ferry port at **Bom Despacho** via a coastal road run by small buses and *combi* minivans via the hamlets of **Ponta de Areia** (with good beaches and many *barracas*), **Amoureiras** and **Manguinhos**. Bom Despacho itself is little more than a ferry dock shops and restaurants. Buses to and from Valença arrive and leave from here.

The island's principal town is **Mar Grande** (aka Veracruz). There are many *pousadas* and a cluster of restaurants here, as well as at the beaches of Mar Grande and **Penha**, to the south. Beaches get better and more deserted the further south you go. They include the **Barra do Gil** (backed with holiday homes), the **Barra do Pote** (with a white-sand beach and calm waters) and **Tairu** (deserted during the week and with fine, white sand).

### Bay islands
There are dozens of other islands in the Baía de Todos os Santos. They include the **Ilha do Frades** and the **Ilha do Maré** (with Mata Atlântica forest and tiny fishing villages). These can be visited with organized tours with **Ilha Bela** or **Tatur** (see Tour operators, page 54).

## Ilha de Itaparica

### Nazaré das Farinhas
On the mainland, 60 km inland from Itaparica, Nazaré das Farinhas (population 25,000) is reached across a bridge by bus from Bom Despacho. This 18th-century town is celebrated for its market, which specializes in the local ceramic figures, or *caxixis*. There is a large market in **Holy Week**, particularly on Holy Thursday and Good Friday. From here buses run to southern Bahia. About 12 km from Nazaré (taxi from Salvador US$4.25, bus at 1530) is the village of **Maragojipinha**, which specializes in making the ceramic figures.

**Tip...**
Make sure you have enough reias to pay for your stay, because there are no banks on the island.

## Where to stay

### Ilha de Itaparica

#### $$ Galeria Hotel
*Praia do Sol, Barra Grande, T071-3636 8441,*
*www.galeriahotel10.com.br.*
German/Brazilian-owned *pousada* with
simple tile-floored a/c en suites around a
large pool and a good restaurant.

#### $$ Pousada Arco Iris
*Estrada da Gamboa 102, Mar Grande beach,*
*T071-3633 1130, www.pousadadoarcoiris.com.*
Magnificent though dishevelled 19th-
century building romantically set in a
garden of mango trees.

#### $$ Pousada Canto do Mar
*Av Beira Mar s/n, Praia de Aratuba, T071-3638*
*2244, www.pousadaumcantodomar.com.br.*
Brightly coloured, simple *cabañas* set in a
pretty garden overlooking what is a lively
beach in summer and a quiet beach the rest
of the year. Friendly staff, decent breakfast.

## Restaurants

### Ilha de Itaparica
There are many Bahianas selling *acarajé* in
the late afternoon and early evening, in the
main *praça* and by the pier at Mar Grande.

#### $$ Volta ao Mundo
*Largo de São Bento 165, Mar Grande,*
*T071-3633 1031.*
A good-value buffet restaurant with a fixed
price, all-you-can-eat lunchtime menu.

## What to do

### Ilha de Itaparica
**Tour operators**
Small boats for trips around the bay can
be hired privately at the small port by the
Mercado Modelo in Salvador. A pleasant
trip out to the mouth of the bay should take
1½ hrs as you sail along the bottom of the
cliff. When arranging to hire any boat check

that the boat is licensed by the port authority
(Capitânia dos Portos) and that there are
lifejackets on board.

## Transport

### Ilha de Itaparica
From Bom Despacho there are many buses,
*combis* and taxis to all parts of the island.

#### Bus
There is a bridge on the southwest side
of the island. Buses from mainland towns
such as Nazaré das Farinhas, Valença and
Jaguaribe (a small, picturesque colonial port),
arrive at Bom Despacho.

#### Ferry
The island is connected to the mainland by
bridge or boat. There are regular ferry services
to **Salvador**. The main passenger ferry
leaves from Bom Despacho and runs to the
**Marítimo de São Joaquim** ferry dock (see
page 56). The 1st ferry to Salvador is at 0515
and the last one at 2300, running at intervals
of 45 mins. During the summer months the
ferries are much more frequent. (In Salvador,
buses for **Calçada**, Ribeira, stop across the
road from the ferry terminal; the 'Sabino
Silva– Ribeira' bus passes in front of Shopping
Barra). A one-way ticket for foot passengers
Mon-Fri is US$1, Sat and Sun US$1.20.

There is also a catamaran service
which departs from Bom Despacho
twice daily, US$1.75.

From Mar Grande a smaller ferry (*lancha*)
runs to the **Terminal Marítimo**, in front of
the Mercado Modelo in Salvador. The ferries
leave every 45 mins and the crossing takes
20-40 mins, US$2 return.

#### Taxi
*Combis* and taxis can be rented for trips
around the island but be prepared to
bargain, US$40-50 for a half-day tour.

## Santo Amaro da Purificação and around

Some 73 km from Salvador, Santo Amaro da Purificação is a sadly decaying sugar centre. It is noted for its churches (which are often closed because of robberies), the most famous of which is the **Igreja Matriz Santo Amaro da Purificação** ① *Praça da Purificação, T075-3241 1172, Mon-Fri 0800-1200 and 1400-1700, Sat 0800-1200*, which has a superb painted ceiling by José Joaquim da Rocha. There is also a municipal palace (1769), a fine *praça* and ruined sugar baron mansions including **Araújo Pinto**, the former residence of the Barão de Cotegipe. It is also the birthplace of Caetano Veloso and his sister Maria Bethânia. Other attractions include the splendid beaches of the bay, the falls of Vitória and the grotto of Bom Jesus dos Pobres. There are a number of interesting festivals and craftwork is sold on the town's main bridge. There are no good hotels or restaurants but there are at least 20 buses a day from Salvador to Santo Amaro and onward buses to Cachoeira.

About 3 km beyond Santo Amaro on the BR-420, turn right onto the BA-878 for **Bom Jesus dos Pobres**, a small, traditional fishing village with a 300-year history. There is one good hotel. To get there, take a bus from Salvador's *rodoviária* (four a day, Camurjipe, US$1.75).

## Cachoeira and São Felix

Set deep in the heart of some of the oldest farmland in Brazil, 116 km from Salvador, **Cachoeira** and its twin town, São Felix, were once thriving river ports that provided a vital supply link with the farming hinterland and Salvador to the east. The region was the centre of the sugar and tobacco booms, which played such an important role in the early wealth of the colony. The majestic *saveiro* (a gaff-rigged boat) traditionally transported this produce down the Rio Paraguaçu to Salvador across the bay. These boats can still occasionally be seen on the river. The town was twice capital of Bahia; once in 1624-1625 during the Dutch invasion, and once in 1822-1823 while Salvador was still held by the Portuguese.

With the introduction of roads and the decline of river transport and steam, the town stopped in its tracks in the early 20th century and thus maintains its special charm. As in Salvador, *candomblé* plays a very important part in town life (see box, page 33). Easy access by river from Salvador allowed the more traditional *candomblé* temples to move in times of religious repression. Cachoeira was the birthplace of Ana Néri, known as 'Mother of the Brazilians', who organized nursing services during the Paraguayan War (1865-1870).

It is hard to get lost in Cachoeira as there are only a handful of streets, all spreading out from the river. The centre of the city and best point for orientation is the Praça da Aclamação and the Igreja da Ordem Terceira do Carmo.

There are a few interesting sights in Cachoeira. The **Casa da Câmara e Cadeia** ① *Praça da Aclamação, T075-3425 1018, daily 0800-1200 and 1400-1800, US$1.25, (1698-1712)*, was, for a brief period when Cachoeira was the state capital in 1822, the seat of the governance of Bahia. Upstairs is the town hall (with stern notices saying no shorts or Havaianas allowed). Downstairs is a **Slavery Museum**, housed in the heavy walled dungeon where slaves were imprisoned behind two sets of strong bars. The dungeon has a sad and oppressive atmosphere.

The **Museu Regional de Cachoeira** ① *Praça da Aclamação 4, T075-3425 1123, Mon-Fri 0800-1200 and 1400-1700, Sat 0800-1230, book ahead, US$1.25*, has a collection of period furniture, sacred images and ecclesiastical items, paintings and documents relating to the history of the town. The dark mark on the walls near the staircase at the entrance show where the river reached during the 1989 flood.

The **Santa Casa de Misericórdia** (1734) was the colonial hospital and has a fine church attached. Other churches include: the 16th-century **Ajuda** chapel (now containing a fine collection of vestments) and the convent of the **Ordem Terceira do Carmo**, whose church has a heavily gilded interior; the **Igreja Matriz** ⓘ *R Ana Nery s/n, Tue-Sat 0900-1200 and 1400-1700, Sun 0900-1200, free*, with 5 m high *azulejos*, and a ceiling painting attributed to José Teolfilo de Jesus (who painted at the Bonfim church in Salvador; and **Nossa Senhora da Conceição do Monte**. All churches are either restored or in the process of restoration.

The **Fundação Hansen Bahia** ⓘ *R 13 de Maio, T075-3425 1453, Tue-Fri 0900-1700, Sat and Sun 0900-1400*, has fine engravings by the German artist Karl Meinz Hansen, who was born in Hamburg and lived on the Pelourinho in Salvador during the 1950s. In a series of xylographs he documented the miserable lives of the downtrodden women who prostituted themselves for pennies. The museum itself is the former house of Ana Néri, Brazil's Florence Nightingale who nursed the injured during the Paraguayan War.

There is a strong **woodcarving** tradition in Cachoeira and many of its artists can be seen at work in their studios.

A 300-m railway bridge built by the British in the 19th century spans the Rio Paraguaçu to **São Felix**, where the **Danneman Cigar Factory** ⓘ *Av Salvador Pinto 30, T075-3438 2502, www.terradannemann.com/en, Tue-Sat 0800-1200 and 1300-1700, free guided tours*, can be visited to see hand-rolling in progress. A trail starting near the **Pousada do Convento** leads to some freshwater bathing pools above Cachoeira. There are beautiful views from above São Félix.

## Around Cachoeira

About 6 km from Cachoeira, on the higher ground of the Planalto Baiano, is the small town of **Belém** (the turning is at Km 2.5 on the road to Santo Amaro), which has a healthy climate and is a popular place for summer homes.

**Maragojipe** (population 39,000), a tobacco exporting port, is 22 km southeast of Cachoeira along a dirt road (BA-123); it can also be reached by boat from Salvador. If you visit, look out for the old houses and the church of São Bartolomeu, with its museum. The main festival is **São Bartolomeu**, in August. Good ceramic craftwork is sold in the town. The tobacco centre of **Cruz das Almas** can also be visited, although transport is poor.

## Listings Recôncavo Baiano

### Tourist information

**Cachoeira**
Tourist office
*R Ana Néri 4, T075-3425 1123.*

### Where to stay

**Cachoeira**

**$$ Pousada do Convento de Cachoeira**
*R Praça da Aclamação s/n, T075-3425 1716, www.pousadadoconvento.com.br.*

Refurbished rooms in a historic building in the centre of the town. The best are on the upper floor overlooking a grassy courtyard and have high wooden ceilings and chunky, handsome furniture. Those on the ground floor are simpler in whitewash and tile and some are only fan-cooled.

**$ Pousada d'Ajuda**
*R Largo d'Ajuda s/n, T075-3425 5278.*
Spacious and clean doubles with little corners cordoned off for showers (ask to

see a few rooms, some have saggy mattresses) and dorms for up to 4. Right next to the Igreja da Boa Morte.

### $ Pousada La Barca

*R Inocência Boaventura 37, 200 m downstream of the Praça Aclamação, T075-3425 1070, http://pousadalabarca cachoeira.blogspot.co.uk/.*

Little rooms in a bright orange annexe and public areas decorated with the paintings by the artist owner Cristina. No a/c.

## Festivals

### Cachoeira

**24 Jun  São João, 'Carnival of the Interior.** Celebrations include dangerous games with fireworks, well attended by tourists.
**Mid-Aug  Nossa Sehora da Boa Morte.**
**4 Dec**  A famous *candomblé* **ceremony** at the Fonte de Santa Bárbara.

## What to do

### Cachoeira

Recommended local tour guide **Claudio** (T075-3982 6080). He doesn't speak much English, but is friendly and knowledgeable.

## Transport

### Cachoeira

There are more than 20 daily buses between **Salvador** and Cachoeira (2½ hrs). The quickest way to get back to Salvador is to take a motorbike taxi from Cachoeira to the BR-420 and wait at the bus stop there; buses pass every 15 mins and are up to an hour quicker because they have fewer stops than buses that leave from Cachoeira's town centre.

**Bus**  To **Salvador** (**Camurjipe**) every hour from 0530. To **Feira Santana**, 2 hrs, US$1.75.

# Cocoa &
## Dendê coasts

South of Salvador and the Recôncavo, Bahia descends in a series of glorious beaches, offshore islands and jungly peninsulas, many of them fringed with coral and mangrove or backed by endless kilometres of coconut palms. Sluggish tropical rivers undulate their way across lowland Bahia from the Chapada Diamantina ('diamond mountains') of the interior and interrupt the coastline, while potholed roads connect crumbling colonial towns like Ilhéus and Olivença, which grew fat on the cocoa and dendê oil trade but have since been slowly withering under the tropical sun.

The glorious coast is within easy reach of Salvador and every year an increasing number of tourists are discovering its forgotten fishing villages. The surf mecca of Itacaré is gradually turning chic. The expat community of Morro de São Paulo, on the island of Tinharé, is finding its beach haven is getting crowded; the nightlife here is notoriously lively. Those seeking seclusion should head for the Peninsula de Maraú, a little further south, or to the little-explored wild beaches beyond Una.

Depending on whom you ask, Tinharé is either a single large island separated from the mainland by the estuary of the Rio Una and mangrove swamps, or a mini archipelago divided by estuaries, mangroves and an impossibly turquoise sea. Either way it is stunning: a semi-wilderness of bird-filled Mata Atlântica forest fringed with swaying coconut palms and white-sand beaches that until recently were known only to fishermen and a few intrepid Brazilian beach travellers.

Before the 1990s the main town here, Morro de São Paulo, on the northern tip of the island, was one of the world's great secret tropical island getaways. Now it is rapidly becoming as over-developed as a Thai beach and many of the original fishermen who lived on the gorgeous beaches that line Tinharé have already been relocated. Every beach for 20 km south of Morro town is now backed by hotels and Morro has become a veritable tourist hotspot.

Morro Town itself is dominated by a lighthouse and the ruins of an early 17th-century colonial fort, built as a defence against European raiders. However, this did not stop the Dutch and French using the waters around the island as hiding places for attacks on the Portuguese and even establishing bases here for brief periods of time.

### Morro de São Paulo

Morro sits right at the northern tip of Tinharé. Boats from Salvador arrive at a jetty and travellers enter the town through the stone arch that once marked the gateway to the fortress. The battlements are now largely in ruin, perched on top of the craggy hill in front of a series of little streets that branch off a small colonial *praça*. The main thoroughfare runs south to the town's beaches. Another path runs north to the lighthouse and a ruined lookout post complete with cannon (dolphins can be seen in August) and along the coastal strand to the village of **Gamboa**, which retains a strong local character and which has another magnificent beach. From Gamboa it's possible to visit the **Fonte de Ceu** waterfall; make sure you check the tide times, or ask around for a guide. It's possible to walk or take one of the regular boats that run between Gamboa and Morro every 30-60 minutes (depending on the time of day), US$0.85.

Morro has five beaches; are all idyllic but are quieter the further from town you go. There is swimming in the sea or in the saltwater coral pools that appear at low tide. The beaches are named prosaically: **Primeira** (first), **Segunda** (second), **Terceira** (third), **Quarta** (fourth) and **Quinta** (fifth). There are boardwalks and a heavy build-up of shacks, beach bars, restaurants and hotels all the way to Terceira. Primeira is barely a beach at all and has the bulk of the hotels. Segunda is a party beach and is very popular with 20-somethings. Quinta is the furthest from town and is the quietest with little noise but the gentle lap of the sea. Before deciding to walk all the way to Quinta (1½ to two hours) check the tide times as the beach gets cut off at high tide.

Morro is tiny and the first four beaches are easily negotiable on foot. A walk from town to Quarta Praia takes around 40 minutes. Until 2008 all roads were sand or dirt tracks but there is now a partially paved section between the town and the beaches, and this is plied by regular VW buses, motorbikes and beach buggies.

Morro is expensive between December and March and gets very crowded during public holidays and prices can more than double. Beware of drug dealers and robbery at the busiest times.

## Tourist information

The website www.morrodesaopaulo.
com.br is more useful than the CIT tourist
booth detailed below, and provides lists
of agencies, hotels and other information
in several languages, as well as the latest
boat times.

### Centro de Informações ao Turista tourist booth (CIT)
*Praça Aureliano Lima s/n, T075-3652 1083,
www.morrosp.com.br (in Portuguese only).*

## Where to stay

In Morro de São Paulo, there are many
cheap *pousadas* and rooms to rent near the
Fonte Grande (fountain), but this part of
town does not get a breeze at night.

There are 4 beaches next to Morro town,
which are quieter the further from town you
go. The 1st and 2nd beaches are designated
party areas, with throbbing bars and
shacks selling food and drinks well into the
night. There are only *pousadas* and a few
restaurants on the final 2 beaches. To reach
the beaches turn right at the end of the main
street; there is only 1 trail out of town. You'll
have to walk as there are no cars on the
island; porters can be hired to transport your
luggage to the hotel in a wheelbarrow.

### $$$$ Hotel Vila dos Orixás
*Praia do Encanto, T075-3652 2055,
www.hotelviladosorixas.com.*
A Spanish-run *pousada* on one of Morro's
loneliest beaches with a series of spacious
chalets set in a coconut garden, next to
a pool and overlooking the beach. Very
peaceful and romantic but a 30-min car ride
from town. The hotel runs regular shuttles.

### $$$$ Pousada Catavento
*4th beach, T075-3652 2021, www.
cataventopraiahotel.com.br.*

One of the most luxurious and secluded of
the hotels on the island, with well-appointed
mock-colonial rooms arranged around a
beautiful sculpted swimming pool, a decent
restaurant and good service.

### $$$$ Pousada da Torre
*2nd beach, T075-3652 1038,
www.pousadadatorre.com.br.*
A very tasteful little boutique hotel on
the beachfront which looks particularly
enticing at night when both the building
and the turquoise pool are mood lit under
the palms. The plushest rooms are on the
upper floor, are decked out in jaqueira wood
and raw stone and have balconies with sea
views behind big French windows. Rooms
in the back annexe are a good deal cheaper,
plainer but are large with king-sized beds
and rich wood walls.

### $$$ Agua Viva
*3rd beach, T075-3052 1217, www.
pousadaaguavivamorro.com.br.*
The best rooms in this simple *pousada*
are at the front and have little balconies
overlooking the beach. They have a/c,
fridges and TVs, polished concrete floors
and are decorated with art painted by the
Morro owners.

### $$$ Fazenda Vila Guaiamú
*3rd beach, T075-3652 1035,
www.vilaguaiamu.com.br.*
7 tastefully decorated chalets of various
sizes and styles set in their own tropical
gardens and visited by marmosets,
tanagers and rare cotingas. The hotel has
a spa service with wonderful massage.
The Italian photographer owner runs an
ecotourism project protecting a rare species
of crab, which live in the river that runs
through the *fazenda*. Guided rainforest
walks available. Excellent food. The best
option for nature lovers.

### $$$ Pousada Vistabella
*1st beach, T075-3652 1001,*
*www.vistabelapousada.com.*
Good rooms, all with fans and hammocks.
Rooms at the front have lovely views and
are cooler. The owner Petruska is very
welcoming. Recommended.

### $$ Bizu Aradhia
*3rd beach, T075-3652 1341,*
*www.pousadaaradhia.net.*
Spotlessly clean whitewash and white tile
a/c rooms next to the beach, with space for a
family of 4, small pool, Wi-Fi and Brazilian TV.

### $$ Barra Vento
*3rd beach, T075-3652 1134,*
*www.pousadabarravento.com.br.*
Friendly and locally run *pousada* with slate
floored a/c rooms, decked out with little
more than a bed and fridge, but each has a
small balcony, Wi-Fi and flatscreen cable TV.
Be sure to try the owner's barbecued pizza
and see his collection of different sands from
around the world.

### $$ Coqueiro Do Caitá
*3rd beach, T075-3652 1194, http://*
*pousadacoqueirodocaita.com.br.*
This little 2-storey hotel sits at the end of a
leafy alleyway behind the beach and has
a series of a/c rooms with little more than
a bed and a fan, suites with a jacuzzi and a
small swimming pool.

### $$ Pousada Colibri
*R do Porto de Cima s/n, Centro, near the*
*fountain, Morro de São Paulo, T075-3652*
*1056, www.pousada-colibri.com.*
One of the few that stays cool in this part of
town. 6 apartments with pleasant sea views.
The owner speaks English and German.

### $$ Pousada Farol do Morro
*1st beach, T075-3652 1036,*
*www.faroldomorro.com.br.*
Little huts running up a steep slope. All are
a little small but have a sea view and are

reached by a private funicular railway. The
pool sits perched on the edge of the hill.
Brazilian owned.

### $$ Pousada Grauça
*3rd beach, T075-3652 1099,*
*www.pousadagrauca.com.br.*
Simple but well-kept a/c and fan-cooled
rooms with en suites in concrete *cabañas*
away from the beach. Formerly called the
'Aradhia'. Recommended.

### $$ Pousada Ilha da Saudade
*1st beach, T075-3652 1015,*
*www.ilhadasaudade.com.br.*
Elegant hillside *pousada* with a beautiful
pool with a view, a small gym and deluxe
suites with jacuzzis. Restaurant, bar and
good breakfast.

### $$ Pousada Ilha do Sol
*1st beach, T075-3652 1457, www.*
*minhapousadailhadosol.com.br.*
A big, blocky hotel with modest but well-
kept rooms on long balcony corridors. The
best have sea views. Generous breakfast.

### $ Pousada Timbalada
*2nd beach, T075-3652 1366,*
*www.pousadatimbalada.com.*
A simple but welcoming guesthouse tucked
away down an alley near party central on
the 2nd beach. Small, brightly painted boxy
rooms with hammock terraces and barely
space for a backpack, and attractive raw
stone and terracotta paint public areas.

## Gamboa

### $$$ Village do Dendê
*Gamboa Beach, T075-3653 7104, www.*
*villagedodende chales.yolasite.com.*
Well-appointed small chalets (each with
a kitchenette and space for a family in
2 separate rooms), set in a lovely garden
filled with dendê palms and heliconia
flowers. Right next to the beach.

## Restaurants

There are plenty of restaurants in Morro de São Paulo town and on the 2nd and 3rd beaches. Most of them are good though somewhat overpriced. For cheap eats stay in a *pousada* that includes breakfast, stock up at the supermarket and buy seafood snacks at the *barracas* on the 2nd beach.

### $$ Tinharé
*Down a little set off steps off*
*R Caminha de Praia.*
The food here bursts with flavour, especially the delicious *peixe escabeche* (fresh fish cooked in coconut milk and served in a sizzling cast-iron pot). The portions are so generous they serve 2-3.

### $$-$ Sabor da Terra
*R Caminho da Praia, T075-3652 1156.*
A very popular lunchtime per kilo and à la carte evening restaurant serving great *moquecas* and seafood.

## Bars and clubs

There is always plenty going on in Morro. The liveliest bars are on the 2nd beach where you'll also find the throbbing **Pulsa** nightclub. These tend to get going after 2300 when the restaurants in town empty.

## Festivals

**7 Sep** There is a big festival at Morro with live music on the beach.

## What to do

### Tour operators
There are numerous small agencies offering boat, beach and snorkelling tours around Morro and it's an idea to shop around for the best price; a full day boat tour, for example, costs US$20-30. They include **Puro Prazer** (T075-8176 8038, www.lanchaspuroprazer. com.br), and a cooperative of taxi drivers and operators based at Receptivo (just behind the 2nd Beach) who run tours to Gamboa (US$9), Garapoa village and beach (one of

the island's prettiest, US$25) and day trips to Boipeba (US$25). All prices are per person.

Most tours go in a clockwise direction around Tinharé, visiting Boipeba and the villages to the south (including Moreré), the offshore reef pools for snorkelling, followed by the tiny colonial town of Cairu on the mainland and the shores of the Mangrove-line Rio Cairu, before returning.

## Transport

Details on current flights and ferry times to Morro de São Paulo can be found on www.morrodesaopaulobrasil.com.br.

VW buses, motorbikes and beach buggies leave from the **Receptivo**, a little café that marks the beginning of the road just behind the 2nd and 3rd beaches; it's not hard to find but if in doubt ask for '*Receptivo*' or '*a estrada*'. There are daily transfers to **Boipeba** by Toyota at 0930, bookable through hotels or the many agencies on the island.

**Air** There are several daily direct 20-min flights from the 3rd beach at Morro de São Paulo to Salvador. These cost US$80-130 one way. Times vary seasonally and from year to year but are usually as follows: **Salvador–Morro** (0830, 1230, 1500, 1530), **Morro–Salvador** (0915, 1315, 1600, 1615). Contact **Addey**, T071-3377 1993, www.addey. com.br, **Aerostar**, T071-3612 8600, www. aerostar. com.br, or drop into the airport office next to the landing strip on Morro.

**Ferry** Several companies run catamarans from Morro de São Paulo to the **Terminal Marítimo** in front of the Mercado Modelo in Salvador (US$40, 1½-2 hrs); see page 56. Times vary according to the season and weather but there are usually several a day 0800-1400; check with the tourist office or **Catamarã Gamboa do Morro**, T071-9975 6395. Part of the trip is on the open sea, which can be rough. There are also water taxis.

Modified fishing and speed boats also run from Salvador via Valença (an unprepossessing town on the mainland served by regular buses from Salvador and southern Bahia) and Itaparica. Boats from Morro de São Paulo and Gamboa run to the main bridge in **Valença** (1½ hrs) 5 times a day, US$1.60 (see below). There is also a *lancha rápida* which takes 25 mins and costs US$8. Private boat hire can also be arranged; contact **Jario**, T075-3741 1681, or book through your *pousada*.

There is a port tax of US$0.50 payable at the dock on leaving Morro or Gamboa (though in practice the staff are rarely there).

### Morro via Valença
**Bus** Long-distance buses run from the new *rodoviária* on Av Maçônica. Many buses a day to **Salvador**, 5 hrs, US$6, several companies, including **Aguia Branca**, T075-3450 4400. **São Jorge** to **Itabuna**, 5 hrs, US$3, very slow. For the shortest route to Salvador, take a bus via Nazaré das Farinhas to Bom Despacho (130 km), and take a ferry from there to the São Joaquim ferry terminal. To **Bom Despacho** on **Itaparica**, **Camarujipe** and **Águia Branca** companies, 16 a day, 1 hr 45 mins, US$3.60.

**Ferry** There are boats to **Gamboa** (1½ hrs) and **Morro de São Paulo** (1½ hrs) from the main bridge in Valença, 5 times a day (signalled by a loud whistle). The fare is US$1.60. The *lancha rápida* takes 25 mins and costs US$8. Only Salvador–Valença buses leaving 0530-1100 connect with ferries. If not stopping in Valença, get out of the bus by the main bridge in town, don't wait until you get to the *rodoviária*, which is a long way from the ferry. Private boat hire can be arranged if you miss the ferry schedule. A responsible local boatman is **Jario**, T075-3741 1681; he can be contacted to meet travellers arriving at the *rodoviária* for transfer to Morro. He also offers excursions to other islands, especially **Boipeba**. There is a regular boat from Valença to Boipeba on weekdays 1000-1230 depending on tide, return 1500-1700, 3-4 hrs.

## Ilha de Boipeba

*a low-key alternative to Tinharé island*

Ilha de Boipeba, a few hours south of Morro, is a similar but far quieter island and with less infrastructure. Accommodation is grouped in three places: the little town on the banks of the Rio do Inferno where the ferry arrives; the adjacent beach, Boca da Barra, which is more idyllic; and the fishing village of Moreré, a 30-minute boat ride to the south (only possible at high tide). With just a few simple restaurants and a football field on the beach overlooking a beautiful turquoise bay, life here is tranquil even by Bahian standards.

Expect to pay at least US$20 for a boat to Moreré. Walking along the beaches will take about two hours. Have your camera at the ready, bring sunscreen and go at low tide as there is a river to ford.

### Listings Ilha de Boipeba

#### Where to stay

Accommodation is split between the little town where the riverboat ferry arrives, the adjacent beach, Boca da Barra, which is more idyllic, and the fishing village of Moreré, 30-mins boat ride to the south (high tide only).

**$$$ Pousada Tassimirim**
*Tassimirim Beach (a 20- to 30-min walk south of town), T075-3653 6030, www.ilhaboipeba. org.br/en/tassimirim.html.*

A coconut grove off the beach shades terracotta-roofed bungalows, an al fresco bar, restaurant and pool and a garden visited by dozens of hummingbirds. The price includes breakfast and dinner. Secluded and very tranquil.

### $$$ Santa Clara
*Boca da Barra Beach, T075-3653 6085, www.santaclaraboipeba.com.*
Californian-owned *pousada* with the island's best restaurant and large, tastefully decorated duplex *cabañas*. Very good-value room for 4 (**$** per person). Superlative therapeutic massages available.

### $$$ Vila Sereia
*Boca da Barra Beach, T075-3653 6045, www. ilhaboipeba.org.br/en/vilasereia.html.*
Elegantly simple wooden chalets overlooking the beach. Breakfast on your own private veranda. Very romantic.

### $$ Horizonte Azul
*Boca da Barra Beach, T075-3653 6080, www.pousadahorizonte azul.com.*
Pretty little *pousada* next door to **Santa Clara**, with a range of chalets from very comfortable to fairly simple. The hillside garden is visited by hundreds of rare birds from the nearby Atlantic coast rainforest. Very friendly owners who speak English and French. Lunch available.

### $ Geographic Hostel
*Praça Santo Antônio 12, T075-3653 6104, www.geographicboipeba.com.br.*
This turquoise blue concrete bungalow, set in gardens in Boipeba village has been converted into a small hostel with boxy dorms and doubles, a large sitting area and a terrace. There is Wi-Fi in public areas.

### $ Sete
*Praça Santo Antônio, Boipeba village, T075-3653 6135, www.ilhaboipeba.org. br/sete.html.*

This family-run 3-room *pousada* in the village is one of the cheapest options in Boipeba and offers small but very well-maintained a/c rooms with tiled floors and whitewashed walls decorated with floral prints.

## Restaurants

Boipeba has cheap eats in the town and surprisingly good food at the **Pousada Santa Clara** and the rustic restaurants in Moreré.

### $$ Santa Clara
*Boipeba, see Where to stay, above.*
San Francisco panache in rustic but elegantly decorated tropical surrounds. Come for dinner. Highly recommended.

### $ Mar e Coco
*Moreré, T075-3653 6013.*
Very fresh seafood in idyllic surroundings, shaded by coconuts and next to a gently lapping bath-warm sea.

## Bars and clubs

Nightlife on Boipeba is limited to star-gazing or having a beer in town.

## Transport

**Boat** Day trips to the island run daily from Morro de São Paulo (see page 64) at 0900; book through a travel agent or your hotel. The return journey costs around US$20; you have to pay this even if you are intending to stay on the island. Tractors and 4WDs leave from Morro's 2nd beach every morning at around 0800 (1 hr, US$9), and return at midday; contact **Zé Balacha** (T075-9148 0343), or ask at your hotel.

There is a regular boat from Boipeba to **Valença** on weekdays 1500-1700, 3-4 hrs. Overnight trips to the village are possible. Contact **Zé Balacha**, T075-9148 0343, or book through your *pousada* in Morro or Boipeba.

## ON THE ROAD
### Itacaré beaches north to south

**Do Pontal** Immediately across the Rio de Contas from town and reached by passenger ferry. Long, deserted and stretching all the way to Barra Grande some 40 km away – if you're prepared to swim across rivers and camp out.

**Coroinha** At the harbour, urban and none too clean but with pretty views of the town and the 18th-century church of São Miguel, especially at sunset.

**Da Concha** Urban and with the bulk of the *pousadas*.

**Do Resende** A little bay with powdery white sand, swaying coconut palms and a handful of *pousadas*. 10 minutes' walk from Da Concha.

**Tiririca** The best surf beach in Itacaré, *pousadas* with a beatnik surfer crowd. 10 minutes' walk from Resende.

**Do Costa** A little bay with strong waves and reasonable surf. 10 minutes' walk from Tiririca.

**Do Ribeira** The end of the road from town. Very pretty with calm water and rainforest rising at each end. Beach *barracas* sell fish and snacks and there's a little stream for kids. 10 minutes' walk from Do Costa.

**Prainha** More private and accessible by trail from Ribeira. Good surf. In a protected area (US$1 entry fee). 20-30 minutes' walk from Do Ribeira.

### South to Itacaré

tangled mangroves, fishing villages and surf beaches

#### Ituberá and Camamu

These two towns, which have yet to be overrun by seasonal visitors, are the first stops south on the bus route from Valença. Neither have good beaches but both have access to decent ones by boat. **Ituberá** is a tiny town sitting on a deep inlet; the most beautiful beach in the area, **Barra do Carvalho**, is two hours away by boat.

Some 30 km further south, **Camamu** is tucked away in a maze of mangroves. It is the jumping-off point for the peninsula of **Maraú**, the next stretch of the Bahian coast in line for beach resort development. The town has a handful of pretty colonial buildings, including the 17th-century church of Nossa Senhora da Assunção.

#### Barra Grande and the Peninsula de Maraú

This long thin peninsula, 200 km south of Salvador, 150 km north of Ilhéus, stretches north from the town of Maraú, near Itacaré, towards the southern extremity of the island of Tinharé and is fringed with beautiful beaches along its entire length both on the ocean side and along the beautiful Baía de Camamu. The bay is lined with thick mangrove at its far southern end and sealed at **Tremembé**, with a plunging waterfall that cascades directly into the sea. The main centre of population is the little fishing village of **Barra Grande** at the tip of the peninsula, fronted by a glorious beach and yachts bobbing at the end of a pier. The sandy streets are lined with a handful of *pousadas* and shaded by *casuarina* and palms. Few non-Brazilian tourists make it here.

> **Tip...**
> The website www.barragrande.net has lots of useful information in English.

## Itacaré

Itacaré is a pretty little surfer town at the far end of the Peninsula de Maraú surrounded by glorious forest-fringed beaches. Paulistanos decided it was cool at the turn of the millennium and a handful of beaches are now backed by some of Bahia's most exclusive (and increasingly oversized) resorts, such as **Txai**. Those close to the town itself are more hippy, with an informal surfer-dude feel and a mix of cheaper restaurants and places to stay and more fashionable spots for those swooping in for the evening. Much of the old town remains a simple fishing village whose houses in thick *gouache* shades huddle together under a golden sun around a broad harbour on the banks of the Rio de Contas.

More deserted beaches lie along dirt roads to the south and north. To explore the area to the full you will need a car. If you speak some Portuguese, it's worth taking the time to find your way to one of the smaller places. Itacaré is very busy with Brazilian tourists in high season but receives relatively few international visitors.

## Listings South to Itacaré

### Tourist information

#### Itacaré

**Secretaria de Turismo de Itacaré**
*T073-3251 2134, www.itacare.com.br.*

### Where to stay

#### Ituberá and Camamu

**$$ Rio Acaraí**
*Praça Dr Francisco Xavier, Camamu, T073-3255 2315, www.hotelrioacarai.com.br.*
Ugly modern *pousada* with a pool and restaurant.

**$ Pousada Green House**
*R Djalma Dultra 61 next to the rodoviária, Camamu, T073-3255 2178.*
Very basic and friendly with breakfast and a simple restaurant.

#### Barra Grande and the Peninsula de Maraú
There are plenty of *pousadas* in Barra Grande.

**$$$$ Kiaroa**
*Praia Taipus de Fora, T073-3258 6216, www.kiaroa.com.br.*
The best of the peninsula's resorts, on a glorious beach, with a range of well-appointed rooms and an excellent restaurant, pampering and various organized activities.

**$$$$ Lagoa do Cassange**
*Praia do Cassange (Caixa Postal 23), Camamu, T073-9973 3903, www.lagoadocassange.com.br.*
Cabins in a lawned garden between a wild stretch of beach and a lake populated with dozens of water bird species. A/c rooms have coffee-coloured walls, raw dark wood and wicker furniture. Bright raw cotton bedspreads, scatter cushions and rugs add splashes of colour. All have small verandas hung with hammocks. The hotel practises sustainable tourism by supporting local communities and undertaking some recycling.

**$$$ Taipú de Fora**
*Praia Taipus de Fora, T073-3258 6278, www.taipudefora.com.br.*
Small upscale mini-resort with a good range of activities including diving and kayaking. The beach is glorious, little-known but one of Bahia's very best (and buried here in text so that only discerning readers will discover it!).

**$$ Eco Village Picaranga**
*Rio Picaranga, Peninsula de Maraú, T073-3251 2159, www.piracanga.com.*
A holistic beachside retreat on the south of the peninsula 6 km north of Itacaré, offering treatments, workshops, courses, excursions and alternative weddings.

Profits are shared with the local community. Accommodation is in comfortable thatched-roof chalets and bungalows and there is a large maloca-like community space for meditation and movement, a sauna and a wholefood restaurant.

### $$ El Capitan
*Av Vasco Neto s/n, a block from the beach at the mainland end of the town, 200 m from the pier, T073-3258 6078, www.elcapitan.com.br.*
Cabins in a garden decorated with rusting anchors and nautical bric-a-brac. All are basic in tile and concrete, have terracotta-tile roofs and hammock-slung terraces gathered around a pool.

### $ Meu Sossego
*R Dr Chiquinho 17, Barra town, T073-3258 6012, www.meusossego.com.*
19 plain a/c rooms with fridges a stroll from the beach.

### $ Porto da Barra
*R Beira Mar, T073-3258 6349, http://pousadaportodabarra.wix.com/pousada.*
Family-run *pousada* right on the beach with simple concrete and tile a/c rooms in long annexes. The best are on the upper floor. Decent breakfast. Friendly owner.

## Itacaré
The area is becoming very popular and prices are going up all the time. Book well ahead in high season. *Pousadas* are concentrated on and around **Praia da Concha**, the 1st beach south of the town centre and the river.

### $$$$ Txai Resort
*Praia de Itacarezinho, T073-2101 5000, www.txai.com.br.*
The most comfortable hotel around Itacaré, set on a deserted beach with very spacious and tastefully appointed bungalows overlooking a long, deep-blue pool shaded by its own stand of palms. Excellent spa and a full range of activities including diving and horse riding.

### $$$ Art Jungle
*T073-99975 0007, www.artjungle.com.br.*
A modern sculpture garden with 8 treehouses in the middle of the forest. All have views out to the sea and to the Rio de Contas. There's also a natural sauna and a yoga space. A favourite with celebrities such as Sean Penn, Jade Jagger and Gisele Bündchen.

### $$$ Maria Farinha
*T073-3251 3515, www.mariafarinha pousada.com.br.*
Simple family-run *pousada* in a concrete annexe overlooking a little pool. Pleasant *maloca*-shaped communal breakfast area, quiet and good for families. Disabled access.

### $$$ Nainas
*Praia da Concha, T073-3251 2683, www.nainas.com.br.*
Rooms in these colourful cabins and annexes are simple but comfortable, with little decks, splashes of colour from bedspreads and art and craft decor. They are set in a lush garden close to the beach.

### $$$ Sage Point
*Praia de Tiririca, T073-3251 2030, www.pousadasagepoint.com.br.*
Ocean-front *pousada* with smart wooden chalets in a tropical garden overlooking the sea, each with their own hammock-strewn terraces. Some are a little small but all have wonderful views. The Cuban owner, Ana, speaks English and can organize trips to nearby beaches.

### $$$ Villa Bella
*Praia da Concha, T073-3251 2985, www.pousadavillabella.com.br.*
A modern beach hotel with well-appointed rooms set in duplex garden cabins, decked out with wood-panel floors and sitting over a generous pool in a large lawned garden.

### $$$ Villa de Ecoporan
*T073-3251 2470, www.villaecoporan.com.br.*
Brightly coloured spacious chalets gathered around a charming little pool in a hammock-

filled garden. Between the town and Praia da Concha. Good Bahian restaurant.

### $$$ Vira Canoa
*Praia da Concha, T073-3251 2525, www.pousadaviracanoa.com.br.*
Maroon bungalows overlooking a lush pool in a pretty garden. Each is decorated with arts and crafts and is filled with heavy wood furniture, TVs and iPod docking stations. The restaurant has good seafood and massages are available.

### $$ Estrela
*R Pedro Longo 34, Centro, T073-3251 2006, www.pousadaestrela.com.br.*
A range of well-maintained, pretty duplex chalets and bungalows with rustic wooden fittings and pastel colours on the walls. The *pousada* serves an excellent home-made breakfast with a huge choice. Staff are friendly and services include free Wi-Fi.

### $$ Pousada Tikuna
*R C, Praia da Concha, T073-99851 0106, www.facebook.com/pousadatikuna.*
A handful of mint-green and tangerine terracotta-tile roofed chalets around a little garden visited by marmosets and parakeets. Great breakfast.

### $$ Sítio Ilha Verde
*R Ataide Seubal 234, T073-3251 2056, www.ilhaverde.com.br.*
These bungalows sitting in a verdant, flower-filled garden are painted in warm tones and are stylishly decorated with local arts and crafts. The largest have space for an entire family.

### $ Albergue o Pharol
*Praça Santos Dumont 7, Itacaré, T073-3251 2527, www.albergueopharol.com.br.*
A pleasant, well-kept hostel 10 mins' walk from the bus stop for Ilhéus in the centre of town and offering simple dorms, triples and doubles and public areas with heavy wooden furniture and lacy hammocks.

### $ Pedra Bonita
*R Lodonio Almeida 120, T073-3251 2402, www.itacarehostel.com.br.*
Pleasant little HI hostel with small doubles and dorms (cheaper) in an annexe, a small pool, internet and TV area. Friendly staff.

## Camping

### Tropical Camping
*R Pedro Longo 187, T073-3251 3531.*
A small palm-shaded campsite in the centre of Itacaré town.

## Restaurants

### Itacaré
There are plenty of restaurants in Itacaré, most of them on **R Lodônio Almeida**. Menus here are increasingly chic and often include a respectable wine list.

### $$$ O Casarão Amarelo
*Praia da Coroinha, T073-3251-3133.*
Swiss-owned restaurant in one of the most beautiful colonial buildings in the town. International menu which is good in parts. The fish is always a reliable choice.

### $$ Beco das Flores
*R Lodônio Almeida 134, T073-3251 3121.*
The busiest restaurant in Itacaré, serving good wood-fired pizzas in tastefully decorated surroundings to a well-dressed post-beach crowd.

### $ O Restaurante
*R Pedro Longo 150, T073-3251 2012.*
One of the few restaurants with a *prato feito*, alongside a mixed seafood menu.

## Bars and clubs

### Itacaré
The liveliest bars are **Praça dos Cachorros** and **Mar e Mel** (www.maremel.com.br) on the Praia das Conchas. The **Casarão Amarelo** restaurant (see Restaurants, above) becomes a dance club after 2300 on weekends. There is frequent extemporaneous *forró* and other live music all over the city and most

restaurants and bars have some kind of music Oct-Apr.

## What to do

### Peninsula de Marau
There are excellent 2- to 5-day tours with **Orbitá** (see page 76), leaving from Ilhéus or Itacaré.

**Lagoa Cassange**, see Where to stay, above. Boat trips around the Baía de Camamu (including to the Tremembé waterfalls and to the surrounding islands), trekking along the beaches (including a wonderful 2-day walk between the Praia do Pontal and the Rio Piracanga) and trips to small, traditional fishing villages such as the boat-building community of Cajaíba.

## Transport

### Barra Grande and the Peninsula de Marau
As well as by plane and boat, it's also possible to reach Peninsula de Marau by road from Itacaré.

Access is difficult to many Marau beaches if you don't have a car (and only possible with a 4WD in wet weather), but some can be reached on foot or by taxi/*combi* from Barra Grande. Tractors run from the village to the more remote beaches further south.

**Air** There are scheduled air taxis from the small airport at Barra Grande to **Morro de São Paulo** and **Salvador**.

**Boat** Boats run from Barra Grande to **Camamu** several times a day Oct-Mar and once daily year round (boats: 1 hr, US$1.75; *lancha*: 20 mins, US$9).

### Itacaré
**Bus** At least 4 buses a day buses to **Ilhéus** (the nearest town with an airport), 45 mins-1 hr, US$7 along the newly paved road. To **Salvador**, change at **Ubaitaba** (3 hrs, US$1.75), Ubaitaba–Salvador, 6 hrs, US$12, several daily. The *rodoviária* is a few mins' walk from town and porters are on hand with wheelbarrows to help with luggage.

## Ilhéus and around

*birthplace of the cult Brazilian author, Jorge Amado*

Everyone is happy to point out that Ilhéus (population 242,500) is the birthplace of Jorge Amado (1912) and the setting of one of his most famous novels: *Gabriela, Cravo e Canela* (Gabriela, Clove and Cinnamon, 1958). Amado also chronicled life on the region's cocoa plantations in two novels, *Cacau* (1933), and the much better-known *Terras do Sem Fim* (The Violent Lands, 1942). A later novel, *São Jorge dos Ilhéus* (1944), continues the story.

Ilhéus's history stretches back to the earliest days of Portuguese colonization, when it was one of the captaincies created by King João III in 1534. Today the port serves a district that produces 65% of all Brazilian cocoa. Shipping lines call regularly. There are good views of the city from the **Convento de Nossa Senhora da Piedade**. Most tourists stay for an hour or two before heading north towards Itacaré or south towards Porto Seguro.

The town has a number of sights. The church of **São Jorge** ① *Praça Rui Barbosa*, (1556), is the city's oldest and has a small museum. The cathedral of **São Sebastião** ① *Praça Dom Eduardo*, is a huge, early 20th-century building. In Alto da Vitória is the 17th-century **Nossa Senhora da Vitória**, built to celebrate a victory over the Dutch. The house where Jorge Amado grew up and wrote his first novel is now a small **museum** ① *R Jorge Amado 21, 0900-1600, US$1*. Immortalized by Amado in *Gabriela, Cravo e Canela*, the **Bataclã** ① *Av 2 de*

*Julho 75, T073-3634 7835*, was once a famous bordello and poker palace. It was used by the region's powerful cacão *coroneis* and linked to other parts of the town by a series of secret tunnels, through which (presumably) the macho men would flee in fear of their wives.

## Around Ilhéus

The city beach itself is polluted but the beaches around the town are splendid and increasingly deserted the further you go. North of Ilhéus, two good beaches are **Marciano**, with reefs offshore and good surfing, and **Barra**, 1 km further north at the mouth of the Rio Almada. South of the river, the beaches at **Pontal** can be reached by 'Barreira' bus; alight just after the **Hotel Jardim Atlântico**. Between Ilhéus and **Olivença** are a number of fine beaches, including **Cururupe**, **Batuba** and **Cai n'Água** (in Olivença itself), both popular surf spots. The **Balneário de Tororomba** ⓘ *on the Rio Batuba, 19 km from Ilhéus, bus from São Jorge, Canavieiras or Olivença*, has ferruginous mineral baths.

From Ilhéus, buses run every 30 minutes to **Itabuna** (32 km), the trading centre of the rich cocoa zone; there are also many lumber mills. **Ceplac installations** ⓘ *Km 8, on the Itabuna–Ilhéus road, T073-214 3000, Mon-Fri 0830-1230*, demonstrate the processing of cocoa. Tours of cocoa plantations can be arranged through **Orbitá**, see What to do, opposite, or the **Ilhéus Praia** hotel.

Also at Km 8, the Projeto Mico-Leão Baiano at the **Reserva Biológica de Una** was founded to protect the golden-faced tamarin. This is the wettest part of Bahia, most notably in October. Jeeps leave from the *rodoviária*. The reserve lies along a dirt road and most easily reached on a tour or by public jeep which leave when full from the *rodoviária*. Tours can be organized through **Orbitá** on request; see What to do, opposite.

Beyond Ilhéus, the paved coastal road continues south through **Olivença** and **Una**, ending at **Canavieiras**, a picturesque town which benefited from the cocoa boom. It has several fine beaches worth exploring. A rough road continues from there to Porto Seguro.

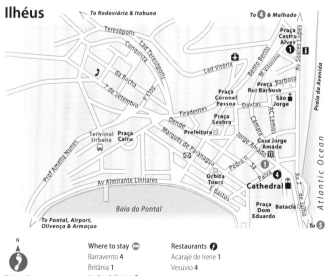

Ilhéus

## Tourist information

### Tourist office
*On the beach opposite Praça Castro Alves.*
A few mins' walk from the cathedral is this office. Staff are friendly and can provide maps (US$1.25, recommended).

## Where to stay

There are plenty of cheap hotels in Ilhéus near the municipal *rodoviária* in the centre; not all are desirable (check for hot-pillow establishments that rent rooms by the hour).

### $$$$ Fazenda da Lagoa
*Rodovia BA-001, Una, T073-9834 2995, www.fazendadalagoa.com.br.*
Carioca Lia Siqueira and Mucki Skowronski's super-chic beach bungalows offer privacy and intimate designer luxury that lures celebrities. However, the real star here is the wilderness landscape: the vast, empty beach and pounding ocean; the adjacent rainforest and mangrove wetlands; and the beautiful river and lake. Unfortunately the owners have little knowledge of natural history, so nature-lovers are advised to organize their own guides (with prior notice) through **Orbitá** in Ilhéus (see What to do, below).

### $$$ Hotel Barravento
*Malhado Beach, R Nossa Senhora das Graças 276, Ilhéus, T073-3634 3223, www.barravento.com.br.*
The smartest hotel in the city. Ask for the penthouse (there is usually no extra charge), which includes breakfast and a fridge.

### $$$ Jardim Atlântico
*Rodovia Ilheus-Olivenca Km 2, Jardim Atlântico, Ilhéus, T073-3632 4711, www.resortjardimatlantico.com.br.*
One of Bahia's few luxurious beach hotels that not only welcomes children but provides kids' clubs, activities and a little

water park. There are tennis courts, sauna, gym and activities for the adults. Rooms have their own little garden and hammock terraces and, thankfully, as the restaurant is a long way away, food is decent.

### $$ Britânia
*R Jorge Amado 16, Ilhéus, T073-3634 1722, www.brasilhcus.com.br/britania_por.htm.*
The best value in the town centre with large rooms in an early 20th-century wooden hotel just west of the cathedral square. Safe area with lots of restaurants.

## Restaurants

Specialities include the local drink, *coquinho*, coconut filled with *cachaça*, which is only for the strongest heads. There are cheap eats from the various seafood stalls on the *praça* and near the cathedral.

### $$$ Bar Vesúvio
*Praça Dom Eduardo, T073-3634 2164, http://barvesuvio.com.*
Next to the cathedral, made famous by Amado's novel, now Swiss-owned. Very good but pricey.

### $ Acarajé de Irene
*Praça Castro Alves.*
Great traditional *acarajé* and other Bahian snacks. Long a local favourite; people come from all over the city just to eat here.

## What to do

### Tour operators
**Orbitá**, *R Marquês de Paranaguá 270, T073-3234 3250, www.orbitaexpedicoes.com.br.*
Organizes adventure trips, visits to Maraú and general tours. The guides are excellent and knowledgeable. The company also operates out of both Itacaré and Una on a pre-arranged pick-up scheme. Transfers can be arranged to Fazenda da Lagoa and throughout Bahia as far as the Chapada Diamantina.

## Transport

**Air** A taxi from town to the airport, 3 km from the centre, in Pontal on the south bank of the river, linked to Ilhéus by bridge, costs US$4. There are flights to **Salvador**, **Belo Horizonte**, **São Paulo**, **Brasília**, **Curitiba**, **Porto Seguro** and **Rio de Janeiro** with GOL, www.voegol.com.br, and **TAM**, www.tam.com.br. Services are often cut back in low season.

**Bus and boat** Most long-distance buses leave from the *rodoviária*, on R Itabuna,

4 km from town. However, the **Itabuna–Olivença** bus goes through the centre of Ilhéus. Several buses run daily to **Salvador**, 7 hrs, US$20 (*leito* US$30, **Expresso São Jorge**), the 0620 bus goes via **Itaparica**, leaving passengers at Bom Despacho ferry station on the island (from where it is a 50-min ferry to **Salvador**). To **Itacaré**, 45 mins-1 hr, US$8. To **Eunápolis**, 4 hrs, US$25, this bus also leaves from the central bus terminal. Local buses leave from Praça Cairu.

**Taxi** Insist that taxi drivers have meters and price charts.

# Discovery
## & Whale coasts

The beaches of the far south of Bahia are among the finest in Brazil: long strands of fine white sand washed by bath-warm sea, or pounded by surf and backed by coconut palms. Some are remote and completely deserted, others are watched over by busy resorts and party towns like Porto Seguro and Arraial d'Ajuda, or forgotten little villages like Caraíva, Corumbau and Curumuxatiba. Pretty Trancoso is perhaps the chicest beach destination north of Punta del Este in Uruguay, with gorgeous beach boutiques.

Offshore, in the far south, are the Abrolhos: an archipelago of rocky coral islands fringed with reef. The islands form part of one of Brazil's most carefully protected marine reserves. The region between Porto Seguro and the islands is one of the best places in South America for seeing humpback whales.

Back on the mainland, Bahia's far south is dotted with indigenous Pataxó villages and has extensive areas of Mata Atlântica rainforest under threat from eucalyptus plantations used to produce toilet paper.

The Discovery Coast takes its name from the first landing by the Portuguese. In AD 1500, Pedro Álvares Cabral became the first European to see Brazil. The sea here was too open to offer a safe harbour, so Cabral sailed his fleet north, to find the harbour he later called 'Porto Seguro' (safe port).

attractive colonial town and resort where Brazil began 500 years ago

Located on the Rio Buranhém, which separates the city from Arraial across the water, modern Porto Seguro (population 140,000) still retains a handful of pretty colonial houses in its attractive dockland area. On the hill above is the higgledy-piggledy Centro Histórico, a peaceful place spread out on a grassy slope, with lovely gardens and panoramic views.

**Porto Seguro**

**Where to stay**
Estalagem Porto Seguro 1
La Torre 11
Navegantes 2
Solar da Praça 4
Solar do Imperador 10
Xurupita 12

Brazil began here; on the far side of the grassy square is a block of Cantabrian marble engraved with the Cross Of The Order Of Christ and marking the spot where the conquistador Gonçalo Coelho formally took the Discovery Coast (and by extension the country) from the Tupiniquim people in 1503. Brazil's oldest church sits behind: the **Nossa Senhora da Misericórdia** ⓘ *Praça Pero de Campos Tourinho, T073-3288 5182, Sat-Wed 0930-1330 and 1430-1700, free*, a squat, functional little building in paintbox blue, built in 1526, with heavy fortified walls and a little scrolled Rococo pediment added like a cake decoration.

Nearby, and sitting in the ruins of a monastery ransacked by the ancestors of the modern Pataxó, is the Jesuit church of **São Benedito** ⓘ *R Dr Antônio Ricaldi s/n*, built in 1549 with even more heavily fortified walls and the church of **Nossa Senhora da Pena** ⓘ *Praça Pero de Campos Tourinho s/n, T073-3288 6363, daily 0900-1200 and 1400-1700, free*, dating from 1708, but built over another fortified 16th-century structure. Inside is what is said to be the oldest statue in Brazil – an undistinguished effigy of St Francis of Assisi. Next door is the sacred art museum and former jail – the handsome 18th-century **Casa de Câmara e Cadêia** ⓘ *Praça Pero de Campos Tourinho s/n, T073-3288 5182, daily 0900-1700, free*.

# ON THE ROAD
## The Pataxó

*"This is our land. You have to respect the land you are walking on because it is ours. When you arrived here this land was already ours. And what did you do to us? You stopped our progress with riot squads, gunfire and tear gas. With our blood we commemorate once more the Discovery of Brazil . (Pataxó indigenous leader during the response to the celebration of Brazil's discovery in 2000.)*

The Pataxó are descendants of the Gê speaking warrior tribes who lived in the mountains along the Bahian coast, and who inflicted the heaviest defeats on the Bahian Portuguese in the first years of the colony. Since contact was made the tribe have suffered greatly. The greatest destruction was in 1951 when one of the most important villages was, ostensibly, caught in a gun battle between bandits and police. Hundreds of Pataxó, including women and children, were murdered.

The Pataxó had long been campaigning to have their tribal lands in the Monte Pascoal national park returned to them. The battle was part of a concerted and ongoing effort to rid the Pataxó of their ancestral lands. In 1961 the federal government converted 22,500 ha of land traditionally occupied by the Pataxó into the Monte Pascoal National Park. The Pataxó were violently evicted. Much of their territory was later ceded to big landowners for farming cacau and planting eucalyptus. On 19 August 1999, numerous indigenous Pataxó people set up camp at the national park, declaring that Monte Pascoal belongs to the Patoxó and demanding the transformation of what the authorities call Monte Pascoal National Park into an indigenous park, the land of the Pataxó, to preserve it and to rehabilitate it . Another Pataxó group, the Pataxó Hã-Hã-Hãe, were treated equally badly. By the 1970s they had been shunted around from one piece of land to another as successive farmers and land speculators moved into the area, eventually settling on the São Lucas ranch where they were denied proper access to drinking water and consistently persecuted.

Whilst prospects remain bleak for the Pataxó they continue to fight to preserve their cultural identity. In the new millennium, two remarkable Pataxó sisters began a cultural renovation project in their village of Jaqueira. They reintroduced the Pataxó language, traditional agricultural methods and implemented an ecotourism project to provide income for the community. Young Pataxó people have found new pride in their culture rather than leaving the community.

A visit to Jaqueira is one of the highlights of a journey through southern Bahia. The Pataxó continue to lobby for the right to live on their ancestral lands. The World Rainforest Movement have details on their latest effort (www.wrm.org.uy) and provide international support for their campaign. For further information see http://pib.socioambiental.org/en/povo/pataxo-ha-ha-hae and, in Portuguese only, www.indiosonline.org.br/novo.

## Tourist information

**Secretária de Turismo de Porto Seguro**
*R Pero Vaz de Caminha 475, Centro, T073-3288 3708, www.portosegurotur.com.br.*
The tourist office has information on tours. Alternatively, contact **Portomondo** or **Pataxo Turismo** (see What to do, below).

## Where to stay

Prices rise steeply Dec-Feb and Jul. Off-season rates can drop by 50%, negotiate the rate for stays of more than 3 nights. Room capacity is greater than that of Salvador. Outside Dec-Feb, rooms with bath and hot water can be rented for about US$100 per month.

There are no hotels of character on the beach; all are huge, brash affairs that look like they belong in 1970s Benidorm. The best beach boutiques are in Trancoso or Arraial, but Porto is better value than either if you opt to stay in town.

**$$$$ La Torre**
*Av Beira Mar 9999, Praia do Mutá, T073-2105 1850, www.resortlatorre.com.*
One of the best big beach resorts in Porto, close to the barraca action on the thronging Praia Mutá. Rooms range from spacious family suites with sea views to boxier options for 2. There's restaurant (low-lit for courting couples in the evening) and a big, sculpted pool. Cheapest rates are through the internet and are inclusive of meals, drinks (only Brazilian alcoholic drinks are provided) and sport activities. The hotel provides enterntainment for adults and children, from light tree-top and zip line adventures and organized play times to ultralight scenic flights and scuba diving. Facilities include a sauna, gym, tennis courts and volleyball, together with regular free transfer to your barraca at the beach, and to the airport.

**$$$$ Xurupita**
*Rua B 25, Taperapuã, T051-4042 3940, www.xurupita.com.*
This is one of the few Porto Seguro resort hotels which doesn't feel like a brash 1970s throwback. Annexes of plain, rooms given splashes of colour from big floral murals and furnished with dull catalogue furniture sit on a shady lawn surrounded by lush Atlantic coastal rainforest. Some have views out over the coast (which is just over 1 km away). The hotel runs transfers to the beach and into town and has a pool, restaurant and a sports centre with gym coaching, squash and tennis.

**$$$ Solar do Imperador**
*Estr do Aeroporto, T073-3288 8450, www.solardoimperador.com.br.*
Well-appointed, spacious and modern a/c rooms in mock colonial style with en suites and balconies in a medium-sized resort hotel on the road to the airport. Large pool and wonderful views from the upper deck in the public area.

**$$ Estalagem Porto Seguro**
*R Mcal Deodoro 66, T073-3288 2095, www.hotelestalagem.com.br.*
Terraced rooms in a deep blue colonial house in the town centre. Great atmosphere and a stroll from nearby restaurants. The hotel can help with tours and transfers.

**$$ Hotel Navegantes**
*Av 22 de Abril 212, T073-3288 2390, www.portonet.com.br/navegantes.*
Simple, plain white wall and tile floor a/c rooms, with en suites and TVs, crowding over a little pool and concrete deck in the centre of town.

**$$ Solar da Praça**
*R Assis Chateaubriand 75, Passarela do Álcool, Centro, T073-3288 2585, www.pousadasolardapraca.com.br.*

Pretty little renovated colonial townhouse with a range of basic but well-kept rooms dominated by a bed. Some with a/c and en suites in an adjacent annexe. Opt for those on the upper floors as they are less musty. The staff can organize trips.

## What to do

**Pataxo Turismo**, *Shopping Rio Mar, loja 3, Passarela do Alcool, T073-3288 1256, www.pataxoturismo.com.br.* An excellent little tour operator offering light adventure trips throughout the region including to Pataxo communities, Monte Pascoal, whale watching and diving around the Abrolhos and to the Jequitinonha delta.

## Transport

**Air** The **airport** is on Estrada do Aeroporto s/n, T073-3288 1880, 2 km from central Porto Seguro. A taxi to the airport (T073-3288 1880) from the riverside ferry in Porto Seguro costs US$5. There are flights to **Belo Horizonte**, **Rio de Janeiro**, **Salvador**, **São Paulo**, **Ilhéus**, **Brasília**, **Curitiba** and **Vitória** in high season with **GOL Tam**, **Azul** and **Passaredo**.

**Boat** Boats cross the river to **Arraial d'Ajuda** on the south bank, 5 mins, US$1 for foot passengers, US$3 for cars, every 30 mins day and night.

**Bus** During Brazilian holiday times, all transport is packed. Buses run throughout the city from the waterfront to the old *rodoviária* near the port every 30 mins, US$0.50. Regular buses run along the seafront from Praça dos Pataxós to the northern beaches, or take a bus to **Porto Belo** or **Santa Cruz Cabrália** from the port.

For beaches south of the Rio Buranhém, see Arraial d'Ajuda (see page 85) and points further south.

The *rodoviária*, 2 km west of the centre, on the road to Eunápolis, receives direct buses from Ilhéus, Salvador, São Paulo and Rio de Janeiro (direct bus at 1600). The *rodoviária* has cafés and snack bars. Taxis charge US$6 to the town or ferry (negotiate at quiet times).

Buses for **Caraíva** via Trancoso leave from the ferry dock in the town centre (at 0700, 1130 and 1530, 3-4 hrs) with an additional service via Eunápolis and Itabela. There are services every half hour or so from the other side of the ferry dock in Arraial d'Ajuda to **Trancoso**. Buses for **Santa Cruz Cabrália** go via Eunápolis (6 daily, 1 hr from Eunápolis).

To **Eunápolis** (change here for destinations along the southern coast and for fast and frequent services to **Trancoso** and **Santa Cruz Cabrália**), every 20 mins, 1 hr 20 mins, US3. **Teixeira de Freitas** (for Caravelas, many more buses to **Teixeira** from Eunápolis), 3 daily, 4-5 hrs, US$15, To **Santa Cruz Cabralia** (for Santo André) **Rio de Janeiro**, 2 daily, direct, the late afternoon executive service is the best at 1700, US$65, 20 hrs (very cold a/c, take warm clothes); or change at Eunápolis. To **São Paulo**, 2 daily, 25 hrs, US$75 better to go to Rio then take the Rio–São Paulo express. To **Salvador** (**Águia Branca**), 3 daily, 11 hrs, US$50. To **Vitória**, 6 daily, 10 hrs, US$40. To **Ilhéus** (for **Itacaré**), 4 daily best early morning and lunchtime, 5½ hrs, US$20.

**Car hire** Several companies at the airport, including **Localiza**, T073-3288 1488 (and R Cova da Moça 620, T073-3288 1488), and **Nacional**, T073-3288 4291.

Heading north of town, on the BR-367 to Santa Cruz Cabrália (known as Avenida Beira Mar), are a string of pretty beaches backed by Brazilian package hotels. The best beaches are at Itacimirim, Curuípe, Mundaí and Taperapuã, which have some lively *barracas*.

A few kilometres before Cabrália, is the tourist village of **Coroa Vermelha** at the site of Cabral's first landfall. A cross marks the spot where the first Mass was celebrated – lost in an array of unitidy beach bars and tacky souvenir shops. Buses from Porto Seguro take about 20 minutes.

# Around Porto Seguro

### Jaqueira Pataxó village

Some 8 km north of Porto Seguro, the beautiful and inspiring Pataxó indigenous reserve of Jaqueira is well worth a visit. Its traditional houses lie in the heart of a stand of indigenous-owned rainforest. All the food is either grown or hunted using traditional techniques. And a small craft shop selling beautiful ceramics, sacred incense and art provides extra revenue. The project was conceived by two impressive Pataxó sisters who despaired at the loss of Pataxó culture in the villages of southern Bahia. Their ecotourism and cultural recuperation model has completely rejuvenated Pataxó culture. Young people are speaking their own language again and rediscovering their identity. It is possible to visit or even stay in the village. Trips can be organized with **Pataxo Turismo** or **Portomondo** (see pages 82 and 95), which works closely with the Pataxó, or through **Terra Morena** in Santo André (see Where to stay, below).

### Estação Veracel Vercruz

*Rodovia BR-367 Km 37, T073-3166 1535/8802 0161, www.veracel.com.br, pre-booking necessary for visits Tue and Thu 0830-1630 and Sat 0830-1130.*

This 6000-ha private reserve, halfway between Santa Cruz Cabrália and Porto Seguro, is one of the best locations in southern Bahia for wildlife and birdwatching. There are some 307 species of birds (with 21 threatened or endangered species and 32 endemics) and 40 mammals, including tapir, jaguar, thin-spined arboreal porcupine, brown howler monkey, Geoffroy's marmoset, crested capuchin and coastal black-handed titi monkey. There are scores of reptiles and amphibians and birdwatching is excellent, with rare species such as the red-billed curassow and banded and white-winged cotingas. This is one of the few locations outside the Amazon where harpy eagles are known to nest. Specialist birding tours are available with **Ciro Albano** (see What to do, below). Visits can be organized through **Mata N'ativa Travel** (see page 95).

### Santa Cruz Cabrália and Santo André

About 10 minutes north of Coroa Vermelha (25 km north of Porto Seguro), Santa Cruz Cabrália is a delightful small town at the mouth of the Rio João de Tiba. It has a lovely beach, river port, and a 450-year-old church with a fine view.

A 15-minute river crossing by ferry takes you to a dirt road on the opposite bank and onward to the small town of **Santo André,** where the German football team famously had their training camp. It's a peaceful place with a handful of little *pousadas*, a long coast of mangrove forests and sweeping beaches cut by rivers. Offshore are a series of sandy shoals surrounded by coral and offering great snorkelling. Come very early to avoid tour boats. Trips can be organized through **Terra Morena** (see Where to stay, below). Hourly buses run between Santa Cruz and Porto Seguro (23 km). *Pousadas* in Santo André will collect travellers from their side of the river.

Beyond Santo André the coast is less visited and wilder, eventually reaching the Jequitinhonha river delta, which is dotted with islands, empty sand flats and extensive mangrove forests. It is a wild and beautiful place. Visits can be organized through **Terra Morena** in Santo André (see Where to stay, below).

## Listings North of Porto Seguro *map p83*

### Where to stay

#### Santa Cruz Cabrália and Santo André

**$$$$ Toca do Marlin**
*Estr BA-001, Km 40.5, Santo André, T073-3671 5041, www.tocado marlin.com.br.*
One of the most luxurious beach resorts in South America, with spacious a/c *cabañas* next to a ranch overlooking a quiet, beautiful beach some 50 km north of Porto Seguro. Excellent food and excursions.

**$$$ Baía Cabrália**
*R Sidrack de Carvalho 141, centro, T073-3282 8000, www.baia cabralia.com.br.*
Medium-sized family resort with a large pool, sauna and gym.

**$$$-$$ Terra Morena**
*T073-3761 4060, www.terramorena.net.*
One of the loveliest smal *pousadas* in southern Bahia. Rooms in brick cabanas

in the lawned garden are simple, but the public areas overlook a beautiful stretch of the coast, the cooking is superb and the massages and treatments in the small spa are as soothing as the gentle Bahian breeze. Very warm and attentive service from the arty family who run the resort and the best boat trips north of Porto Seguro.

**$$ Victor Hugo**
*Villa de Santo André, Km 3, Santa Cruz Cabrália, T073-3228 1880, www.pousadavictorhugo.com.*
Smart, tastefully decorated little *pousada* right on the beach on the edge of an environmentally protected area.

### What to do

#### Estação Veracel Veracruz
**Ciro Albano**, *www.nebrazilbirding.com.*
The best birding guide for the northeast

of Brazil offering tips to birding and wildlife sites, including Estação Veracruz, Canudos and the Chapada Diamantina. Trips to the reserve can also be organized through **Mata Nativa Travel**, see page 95.

## South of Porto Seguro

*fashionable beach towns and some of Bahia's most beautiful beaches*

### Arraial d'Ajuda

A five-minute float across the Rio Buranhém from the docks at Porto Seguro brings you to Arraial d'Ajuda, a pretty little colonial village-turned-beach-party town and a more popular base for travellers than

**Tip...**
Arraial is one of the best places in Brazil to learn capoeira; see box, page 86.

Porto. Arraial is an ideal place to get stuck, with a string of gorgeous beaches that begin at the mouth of the river at **Araçaipe** and continue south indefinitely. The little hotels behind the sand are on a far smaller scale than Porto's package-tourist towers and cater to shallow as well as deep pockets. The town itself many pleasant little bars and restaurants; all of which are easily accessible on foot. At Brazilian holiday times (especially New Year and Carnaval) it is very crowded, almost to bursting point.

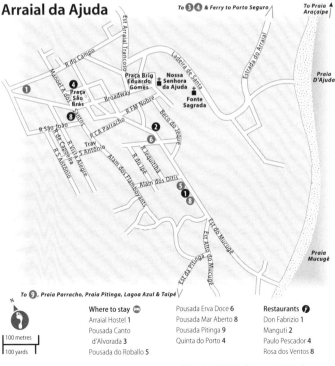

**Arraial da Ajuda**

To ❸❹ & Ferry to Porto Seguro
To Praia Araçaipe
Est Arraial Trancoso
R do Campo
Ladeira de Santa
Estrada do Arraial
Praça Brig Eduardo Gomes
Nossa Senhora da Ajuda
Praia D'Ajuda
Praça São Brás
Broadway
Fonte Sagrada
R F M Nobre
Manoel A dos Santos
R CA Parracho
Beco do Jeque
R São João
❷
R de Capoeira
R Vista Alegre
Trav S Antônio
❻
R Jequitibá
R do Ipê
Alam dos Flamboyants
Alam dos Oitis
❺❶
❽
Est do Mucugê
Praia Mucugê
Est Alto do Mucugê
Estrada Pitinga
To ❾, Praia Parracho, Praia Pitinga, Lagoa Azul & Taipé

N
100 metres
100 yards

**Where to stay** 🛏
Arraial Hostel **1**
Pousada Canto d'Alvorada **3**
Pousada do Roballo **5**

Pousada Erva Doce **6**
Pousada Mar Aberto **8**
Pousada Pitinga **9**
Quinta do Porto **4**

**Restaurants** 🍴
Don Fabrizio **1**
Manguti **2**
Paulo Pescador **4**
Rosa dos Ventos **8**

## ON THE ROAD

## Capoeira

Capoeira is the most visually spectacular and gymnastic of all martial arts and the only one to have originated in the Americas. Salvador is the capoeira centre of Brazil and seeing a fight between good Bahian capoeristas is an unforgettable experience. Fighters spin around each other in mock combat, never touching but performing a series of lunges, kicks and punches with dizzying speed and precision. Some wear razor blades on their feet. A ring or *roda* of other capoeristas watches, clapping, singing and beating time on a *berimbau* and hand-held drum. Every now and then they exchange places with the fighters in the centre of the ring.

Although many claim that capoeira derives from an Angolan foot-fighting ritual, this is incorrect. Capoeira originated in Brazil and there is strong evidence to suggest that it was invented by indigenous Brazilians. Padre José de Anchieta, a 16th-century ethnologist, makes an aside in his 1595 book *The Tupi Guarani Language* that the 'Indians amuse themselves by playing capoiera' and other Portuguese explorers like Martim de Souza recall the same. The word capoeira itself comes from Tupi-Guarani and means 'cleared forest' and the postures, including many of the kicks, spins and the crouching position taken by those in the circle are all Brazilian-Indian. It was in indigenous capoeiras that the fight was passed on to African plantation slaves who modified them, added African chants and rhythms and the *berimbau*; an instrument probably brought to Brazil from West Africa. The art was used as a weapon against the soldiers of the enslaved African king Zumbi who established the Americas' only free slave state just north of Bahia in the 1700s.

The town centre is clustered around the pretty 16th-century church of **Nossa Senhora da Ajuda** (1549), which sits high on a cliff, affording great views of the palm-covered coast. The principal streets extend off the square in front of the church. The largest, which is lined with shops, bars, restaurants and *pousadas*, is called Broadway. There's a party here or on one of the beaches almost every night in high season.

Arraial's beaches are splendid: some pounded by surf, others are little bays gently lapped by an Atlantic tamed by an offshore reef. Most have *barracas* selling good simple seafood and chilled drinks, and playing music. From north to south they are as follows. **Araçaípe** is popular with families and day visitors from Porto, and has several pretty beach hotels and *pousadas*. **D'Ajuda** is in front of the town and has a small protected area. **Mucugê** just to the south of Arraial, has good surf, plenty of beach *barracas* for *forró* and *lambada* parties in the summer. To reach these, take Rua da Praia out of town. South beyond Mucugê is **Parracho**, which is popular for windsurfing and kayaking (rental available); followed by **Pitinga**, with strong waves breaking on the offshore reef creating some decent surf. The penultimate beach is **Lagoa Azul**, backed by cliffs, with gorgeous sand and strong surf. Few make it to the beach farthest south, **Taipé**, an hour's walk from Arraial. It is backed by sandstone cliffs and has glassy water and a handful of *barracas*. At low tide it is possible to walk to from Taipé to Trancoso (see below) along the beach via the village of **Rio da Barra**; allow two hours. A dirt road behind the beach follows the same route and is plied by taxis and cars; it is easy to hitch a lift.

## ON THE ROAD

## Whale watching in Bahia

Between July and December, southern Bahia is visited by hundreds of humpback whales which calf in the waters between Porto Seguro and the Abrolhos archipelago. Boat trips can be organized with tour operators in Arraial or Trancoso (see Portomondo or Mata N'ativa Travel, page 95) or the whales can be seen on a trip to the Abrolhos islands (see page 89).

Humpbacks (*baleia jubarte* in Portuguese) measure between 12 m and 15 m and weigh 25 to 40 tons (with the females being larger than the males). They are black on the dorsal (upper) side, and mottled black and white on the ventral (under) side. Occasionally the whales breach, exposing their huge flippers and broad and barnacle-encrusted heads. These have distinctive rounded, bump-like knobs, each containing at least one stiff hair, thought possibly to assist the whale in detecting movement.

The whales feed on small shrimp-like crustaceans called krill, and small fish, eating around 1½ tons a day. These are sieved through 270-400 fringed overlapping plates, or baleen, hanging from each side of the upper jaw.

Humpbacks are found in all the world's oceans and follow a regular migration route, spending summer in polar or temperate waters and winter in the tropics where they mate and give birth. Males sing complex songs lasting from 10-20 minutes, repeated continuously for many hours and changing gradually every year. Scientists have found that whales in the North Western Atlantic population sing one song and those in the North Eastern Pacific a different one.

The International Whaling Commission (IWC) gave humpbacks worldwide protection status in 1966, although Japan still illegally hunts them. Humpback whales number about 30,000-40,000 today, some 30-35% of the estimated original population.

The **Humpback Whale Institute** (Instituto Baleia Jubarte, Rua do Barão do Rio Branco 26, Centro, Caravelas, T073-3297 1340, www.baleiajubarte.org.br, Monday-Friday 0900-1200 and 1400-1800, Saturday 0900-1200), has information on humpbacks, their conservation in Abrolhos and where else to see them in Brazil.

## Trancoso

In the last five years this once-sleepy little village, 15 km south of Arraial, has become Bahia's chicest beach destination, beloved of the Brazilian and international jet-set for its combination of low-key atmosphere and high-fashion labels. The coolest São Paulo names fill the tiny shopping centre and the town and beaches are dotted with smart designer boutiques and haute-rural restaurants offering the best food outside Rio de Janeiro and São Paulo. Celebrities come here to be recognized only by those they wish to be recognized by, especially the Mario Testino set. Despite its status, Trancoso remains a simple little town at heart, and herein lies its charm.

It is glossy but intimate, with life focusing on the **Quadrado**, a long grassy square where locals play football in the evening. The square is crowned with the little whitewashed 17th-century church of **São João Batista**, and lined with colourful little *casas*, each housing a bikini boutique, crafts shop, fashionable restaurant, bar or guesthouse. The houses are particularly enchanting at night, when they contrast with the dark indigo canvas of the rainforest, under a dome of stars.

Below the Quadrado are a stretch of beaches extending away to the north and south. The most famous and the closest to town are **Praia do Trancoso** and **Praia dos Nativos**, both washed by gentle waves, with coral far offshore and a cluster of chic-shack *barracas* that host parties for the designer-label brigade during the summer months. **Coqueiros**, across the little river to the north is quieter, with one simple restaurant and a view. To the south beyond Trancoso beach are **Rio Verde**, with a little river, and beyond it **Itapororoca** a deserted beach with just a few very expensive houses and good clear-water snorkelling.

## Espelho

A 50-minute drive along the dirt road to Caraíva, Espelho is one of the state's most beautiful beaches: a glassy bay fringed with white sand and rocks with a handful of very plush beach hotels and a delightful restaurant. The Caraíva bus will drop you at the turn off to the beach, from where it is a 5-km walk; or you can visit as part of a tour with an agency such as **Mata N'ativa Travel**, either by car or boat.

## Caraíva

This incredibly peaceful, atmospheric fishing town, 65 km south of Porto Seguro, is on the banks of the Rio Caraíva. Electricity (during the daytime only) and hot water were only installed in 2008 and the streets are sand so there are no cars. The marvellous beaches here make a real escape from Trancoso, Arraial and Porto Seguro. Despite

> **Tip...**
> Flip-flops are best for walking along the sandy streets, and take a torch as it is very dark at night.

difficult access, Caraíva is becoming increasingly popular; high season is December to February and July. There are plenty of cheap *pousadas* and restaurants along the rustic sandy streets. Most bars have live *forró* in the summer.

There is a good walk north to **Praia do Satu** (where Señor Satu provides an endless supply of coconut milk), or 6 km south to a rather sad Pataxó indigenous village; watch the tides as you may get cut off. Horses can be hired through any of the *pousadas* and buggy rides to Corumbau (from where buses connect to Cumuruxatiba) can be organized from the town square with the Pataxó (US$30). Or you can walk the 12 km along the beach to the river that separates Caraíva's last beach with Corumbau village; there is a boatman here for crossings (US$1.25, 10 minutes). Boats can be hired (US$30-80 per day, depending on whether it's a simple boat or a plush speedboat) at the river port in Caraíva for excursions to Caruípe Beach, Espelho, snorkelling at Pedra de Tatuaçu reef or Corombau (take your own mask and fins), or for trips up the beautiful river Rio Caraíva which gets into rainforest some 10 km inland. **Prainha** river beach, about 30 minutes away, and mangrove swamps can also be visited by canoe or launch. Stand-up paddle boards can be hired through *pousadas* or boatmen on the waterfront.

## Parque Nacional de Monte Pascoal
*16 km north of Itamaraju, Itamaraju, T073-3281 2419.*

The national park was set up in 1961 to preserve the flora, fauna and birdlife of the coast where Europeans first landed in Brazil. There is a bus from Itamaraju at 0600 (Monday to Friday); taxis run from Itamaraju cost around US$40 for the round trip including waiting time. Or the park can be visited with a tour group such as **Portomondo** or **Mata N'ativa Travel** (see page 95).

## Corumbau

This tiny fishing village sits on a little promontory of land that sticks out into the deep blue of the Bahian Atlantic. It's a one-beach buggy town, with a tiny church and a handful of very cheap *pousadas* and restaurants; but it is fringed with beaches every bit as gorgeous as any of those around Caraíva or Trancoso. There is great snorkelling from the beach to the south of town. Foreigners are few and far between, except for a handful who come to stay at the exclusive resorts to the south of the town.

Corumbau is not easy to reach. The best way is to organize a transfer with a boatman in Caraíva or an agency in Porto Seguro or Trancoso (see What to do, page 82, and below). However, it is possible to get here by catching the bus to Caraíva and then either sharing a buggy ride from the main square (US$30) or walking the 12 km to the river and catching the ferry boat (see Caraíva Transport, below). There is one daily bus from Itamaraju.

## Caravelas

Continuing south, Caravelas is a pleasant little town on the banks of the Caravelas estuary surrounded by mangroves. Most travellers visit only to stay overnight en route to the Abrolhos Islands, because Caravelas is the port of departure. While there is little to see in the town itself and the town beach is nothing special, there are fine white-sand beaches immediately to the north (see Around Caravelas, below).

Caravelas is well known for its Catholic festivals, which attract thousands of pilgrims. It was a major trading port in the 17th and 18th centuries – as the town's name attests – taken from the Portuguese sailing boats whose technology opened up the world to Lisbon. It is now slowly developing as a resort for Brazilian tourism. There is a helpful tourist information office, **Centro de Visitantes** ⓘ *Barão do Rio Branco 281*.

### Around Caravelas

The best beaches near Caravelas are about 10 km away at the fishing village of **Barra de Caravelas** (hourly buses).

Other beautiful beaches nearby include **Iemanjá**, pounded by good surf, **Zeloris Beach** (deserted and accessible through *fazendas* by taxis which have to turn right off the BA-001 highway) and **Praia Ponta da Baleia** to its north. Praia Ponta da Baleia is a wild palm-shaded stretch of pearl white sand sitting in a small protected area on a headland northwest of Zeloris and reachable only via a rough coastal road running northwest out of town for around 15 km or along the sand from Zeloris itself.

Through local hotels it's easy to organize boat trips on the **Caravelas river delta**, an extensive, pristine mangrove-lined wetland south of town with stretches of gallery forest rich in flora and fauna. The area is rich in wading birds and dotted with sandy islands sitting in crystal-clear water swimming with colourful fish. The islands include Cassumba, Pontal do Sul and sandbanks, and a handful of tiny sandbanks in front of Grauçá beach.

### Parque Nacional Marinho dos Abrolhos

Abrolhos, 70 km east of Caravelas, is an abbreviation of *Abre os olhos*, 'Open your eyes', from Amérigo Vespucci's exclamation when he first sighted the reef in 1503. Established in 1983, the park consists of five small islands: **Redonda**, **Siriba**, **Guarita**, **Sueste** and **Santa Bárbara**, which are volcanic in origin. There are also abundant coral reefs and good diving. Darwin visited the archipelago in 1830 and Jacques Cousteau studied the marine environment here.

The archipelago national park protects the most extensive coral reefs in the south Atlantic with four times as many endemic species than the reefs and atolls in the

Caribbean. There are numerous endemic species, including giant brain corals, crustaceans and molluscs, as well as marine turtles and mammals threatened by extinction and huge colonies of nesting seabirds. In addition, the seas around the islands are one of the most important south Atlantic nurseries for humpback whales, which can always be seen in season. It is possible to dive or snorkel at Abrolhos either on a day trip or on a liveaboard boat; see What to do, below, for details of tour operators. For further information on the archipelago, see www.ilhasdeabrolhos.com.br.

In 2002, the Abrolhos region was declared an area of Extreme Biological Importance by the Brazilian Ministry of Environment, based on the Brazilian commitment to the international Convention on Biodiversity. For more information see **Conservation International** ⓘ *www.conservation.org*. The archipelago is administered by **ICMBio** ⓘ *www.icmbio.gov.br*, and a navy detachment mans a lighthouse on Santa Bárbara, which is the only island that may be visited. Visitors are not allowed to spend the night on the islands, but may stay overnight on schooners.

## Listings South of Porto Seguro *map p85*

### Where to stay

#### Arraial d'Ajuda
At busy times such as **New Year's Eve** and **Carnaval**, don't expect to find anything under US$9 per person in a shared room, with a minimum stay of 5-7 days.

#### $$$ Pousada Canto d'Alvorada
*On the road to the Arraial d'Ajuda ferry, T073-3575 1218, www.cantodalvorada. com.br. Cheaper out of season.*
Pretty, Swiss-run *pousada* facing the beach on the edge of town with 21 cabins, a restaurant, pool, sauna and laundry facilities.

#### $$$ Pousada Pitinga
*Praia Pitinga, T073-3575 1067, www.pousadapitinga.com.br.*
Wooden chalets in a coconut-filled rainforest garden on a hill overlooking the sea. Tranquil atmosphere, great food and a pool

#### $$$ Privillage Praia
*Estrada da Pitinga 1800, Praia Pitinga, T073-3575 1646, www.privillage.com.br.*
This tranquil *pousada* sits in secluded forest overlooking an almost deserted beach 10 mins from Arraial d'Ajuda town. Rooms are less beautiful than the setting – set in concrete chalets and with raw brick walls, tiled floors and heavy wicker furniture. All

have international TV and comfortable king-sized beds and a number have ocean views. The *pousada* has a good restaurant and a pool whose waters appear to merge with the sea.

#### $$$ Quinta do Porto
*Ponta do Apaga Fogo 1, T073-3575 1022, www.quintadoporto.com.br.*
Rooms in long corridors above a smart pool set in tropical gardens right on the river opposite Porto Seguro. Convenient for both Arraial and Porto towns (*combis* from Porto every 10 mins, ferries from Porto every 15 mins), and with an excellent travel agencies for onward excursions. The beach is 10-15 mins' walk.

#### $$ Pousada do Roballo
*Estr do Mucugê, T073-3575 1053, www.pousadadoroballo.com.br.*
Welcoming *pousada* with a set of small rooms, each with a tiny veranda with hammock. Set in pleasant garden surroundings and with a pool.

#### $$ Pousada Erva Doce
*Estr do Mucugê 200, T073-3575 1113, www.ervadoce.com.br.*
Well-appointed chalets and a decent restaurant, set in a lawned garden and with a pool.

## $$ Pousada Mar Aberto
*Estr do Mucugê 554, T073-3575 1153,*
*www.marabertopousada.com.br.*
Pretty little *pousada* with brick chalets
and a pool set on the crest of a hill and
set in lush gardens close to Mucugê Beach
and the centre. At the lower end of the
price category.

## $ Arraial Hostel
*R do Campo 94, T073-3575 1192/1998, www.*
*arraialdajudahostel.com.br. Price per person.*
Smart well equipped modern backpacker
hostel in a large and colourful little house
on the edge of town. Good facilities include
a pool, bar, internet and book exchange.

## Trancoso
Trancoso can be packed out in high season.
Be sure to book ahead. There are no really
cheap rooms.

## $$$$ Etnia
*R Principal, T073-3668 1137,*
*www.etniabrasil.com.br.*
This captivating eco-chic *pousada* a stroll
from the Quadrado is a glossy magazine
favourite, with a series of elegant and
individually style bungalows gathered around
a lush designer pool and set in a tropical
forest garden filled with brilliantly coloured
birds and butterflies. Run with *gaúcho* and
Italian style, panache and efficiency.

## $$$$ Mata N'ativa Pousada
*Estr Velha do Arraial s/n (next to the river*
*on the way to the beach), T073-3668 1830,*
*www.matanativapousada.com.br.*
The best in town for nature lovers and those
seeking a quiet, relaxed retreat. A series of
elegant and romantic cabins are set in a
lovingly maintained orchid and heliconia
garden with a pool by the riverside, which is
a good few degrees cooler than anywhere
else in Trancoso in the heat of the day.
Nothing is too much trouble for the warm-
hearted owners Daniel and Daniela. Both are
knowledgeable about flora and fauna in the

Mata Atlântica rainforest and can organize
wildlife or birdwatching trips throughout
southern Bahia. Good English, Spanish and
Italian. Great breakfast.

## $$$$ Pousada Estrela d'Água
*Estrada Arraial D'Ajuda, Praia dos Nativos,*
*T073-3668 1030, www.estreladagua.com.br.*
An infinity pool with waters melding into
the turquoise sea leads to a light-flooded
living area and a garden with luxurious
faux-fishermen's cottages decorated with
minimalist, clean whites and deep blues.
There is free Wi-Fi throughout and the
hotel follows the PNUMA UN programme
for nature, installing solar power, recycling
and engaging in some small welfare
programmes. The bar is a favourite sunset
cocktail spot.

## $$$$ Villas de Trancoso
*Estr Arraial D'Ajuda, T073-3668 1151,*
*www.villasdetrancoso.com.*
A series of luxurious cabins gathered on
a lawn next to a pool and a relaxed bar
and rustic wood-weight gym area on the
adjacent beach. The duplex suite is perhaps
the most luxurious in the town. American-
run and owned and with a Californian feel.
Can be hot as there isn't much shade.

## $$$$ Capim Santo
*to the left of the main square, T073-3668 1122,*
*www.capimsanto.com.br.*
Friendly, beautifully designed little *pousada*
right on the edge of Quadrado and with a
series of well-appointed rustic chic rooms
and cabins. The restaurant is one of the
best and most romantic in town. Superb
breakfasts and dinners.

## $$$ Pousada Calypso
*Parque Municipal, T073-3668 1113,*
*www.pousadacalypso.com.br.*
Comfortable, spacious rooms, jacuzzis,
a library and sitting area and helpful staff
who speak German and English. Just off
the Quadrado.

## $$ Pousada Quarto Crescente
*R Principal, T073-3668 1014,*
*www.quartocrescente.net.*
About 500 m inland, away from the main
square, on the main road to the beach. With
cooking facilities, laundry and helpful owners
who speak English, German, Dutch and
Spanish. Map, bus times and directions on
the website.

## $$ Pousada Som do Mar
*Beco da Praia dos Nativos, Praia dos Nativos,*
*T073-3668 1812, www.pousadasomdomar.*
*com.br.*
Simple little mock-colonial cubes with
terraces hung with hammocks overlooking
a tiny pool 5 mins' walk from the Nativos
Beach. Internet and Wi-Fi.

## $ Café Esmeralda
*T073-3668 1527, www.trancosonatural.com.*
Tiny white-washed rooms in rather airless
fan-cooled, tile-roofed bungalows right on
the Quadrado. The *pousada* restaurant serves
good breakfast (extra) and some of the
cheapest lunches in Trancoso, and is one of
the few establishments to be locally owned.

## Caraíva

### $$$$ Le Paxa
*Rua da Praia s/n, T073-99926 6621.*
2 rustic chic raw wood cabins set in a garden
in front of the beach, luxuriously decked out
with a huge bed draped in Egyptian cotton,
bric-a-brac collected over a lifetime of
travelling by the Franco-Brazilian owners and
cooled by gorgeous wood shutters letting
the breeze in right off the sea. 80% of the
money from the *pousada* goes to supporting
local community projects. One of the best
places in Bahia.

### $$$ Vila do Mar
*R 12 de Outubro s/n, T073-3668 5111,*
*www.pousadaviladomar.com.br.*
Spacious, stylish airy, wooden *cabañas*
overlooking the beach set on a lawn
around an adult and children's pool.

## $$ Pousada da Praia
*Praia de Caraíva, T073-9985 4249,*
*www.pousadapraiacaraiva.com.br.*
Very simple little boxes with no more than
a bed, a table, chair and wardrobe. Public
areas are furnished more comfortably, with
an outdoor deck area hung with hammocks
and dotted with wicker sofas.

## $$ Pousada Flor do Mar
*R 12 de Outubro s/n, on the beach, T073-*
*9985 1608, www.pousadaflordomar.com.*
Charming beachfront *pousada* with airy
rooms with a view – the best right next
to the beach.

## $$ Pousada San Antônio
*Praia de Caraíva, T073-9962 2123,*
*www.pousadasanantonio.com.br.*
Very simple but colourful fan-cooled rooms
right on the beach and breezy public areas
decorated with marine bric-a-brac and
furnished with wicker chairs and hammocks.

## $$ Pousada Terra
*Praia de Caraíva, T073-9985 4417,*
*www.terracaraiva.com.br.*
Simple cabins on the edge of the town and
on the outskirts of the Monte Pascoal forest.

## Camping

### Camping Caraíva Praia de Caraíva
*Praia de Cariava, T073-2231 4892,*
*www.camping caraiva.com.br.*
Basic but shady plots by the riverside with a
communal cooking area and showers, and a
selection of simple shacks with hard beds ($).

## Corumbau

### $$$$ Fazenda São Francisco
*T011-3078 4411, www.corumbau.com.br.*
Spacious, well-appointed hard wood
and cream cabins gathered around a
pool in a palm-shaded garden 5 mins'
walk from the beach.

#### $$$$ Vila Naia
*T011-3061 1872, www.vilanaia.com.br.*
Tastefully appointed, luxurious bungalows set in a little garden back from the beach. Very popular with fashionable Paulistanos. Intimate and romantic.

#### $$$ Jocotoka Village
*T073-3288 2291, www.jocotoka.com.br.*
Brilliantly coloured, higgledy-piggledy, thatched-roof chalets grouped on a shady lawn between the beach and patchy *restinga* forest. Children under 5 and pets are not permitted.

#### $$$ Pousada Corumbau
*T073-3573 1190, www.corumbau.tur.br.*
It's difficult to miss this big red 2-storey house in tiny Corumbau. There are a range of rooms – from simple concrete huts (with space for up to 4 at a push), to big tiled rooms in the main building. All are homey but decorated in brash colours.

#### $ Villa Segovia
*Corumbau s/n, T073-9986 2305, www. corumbaunet.com.br/sites/vilaseg/.*
There are only 5 small, fan-cooled and barely furnished chalets in this little family-run guesthouse close to the beach. They include breakfast and there are plots for camping out back.

### Caravelas

#### $$ Marina Porto Abrolhos
*R da Baleia, 5 km outside of town, T073-3674 1060, www.marinaportoabrolhos.com.br.*
One of the most comfortable hotels in the region, with a range of individual and family suites housed in faux-Polynesian chalets and gathered in a palm-tree garden around a large pool. Activities include trips to the Abrolhos.

#### $$ Pousada Do Beco Shangri-la
*R 7 de Setembro 219, Caravelas, T073-3297 1590, www.facebook.com/pousadasangrila/.*
Simple *pousada* run by the warm and attentive Marcos and his family. The hotel

can organize trips to the Abrolohos and excursions around Caravelas.

#### $$ Pousada Liberdade
*Av Ministro Adalicio Nogueira 1551, Caravelas, T073-3297 2415, www.pousadaliberdade.com.br.*
Spacious but simple chalets in a large, lawned garden area next to a lake and just outside the town centre. Trips organized to the Abrolhos Islands.

### Restaurants

#### Arraial d'Ajuda
Food in Arraial is pricey and restaurants tend to look better than the dishes they serve. There are numerous *barracas* selling simple seafood, juices and beer on Mucugê Beach, as well as the popular **Barraca de Pitinga** and **Barraca do Genésio** on Pitinga Beach.

#### $$$ Don Fabrizio
*Estrada do Mucugê 402, T073-3575 1123.*
The best Italian in town, in an upmarket open-air restaurant with live music and reasonable wine.

#### $$$ Manguti
*Estrada do Mucugê, T073-3575 2270, www.manguti.com.br.*
Reputedly the best in town, though the food looks like mutton dressed as lamb. Meat, pasta, fish served as comfort food alongside other Brazilian dishes. Very popular and informal.

#### $$$ Rosa dos Ventos
*Alameda dos Flamboyants 24, T073-3575 1271.*
This romantic little spot decorated with arts and crafts by local artists cooks fresh food pulled from their own organic garden and the Atlantic. The menu is quite varied, with dishes like fish slow-roasted in banana leaf, braised lamb and crawfish lobster (which should be ordered 24 hrs in advance).

#### $ Paulo Pescador
*R São Bras 116, T073-3575 1242, www.paulopescador.com.br.*

One of the best options for lunch, with 6 different *pratos feitos* (set meals) to choose from and good fresh seafood. English spoken, good service. The *bobó de camarão* is delicious and it comes in generous portions. Very popular, there are often queues for tables.

## Trancoso

Food in Trancoso is expensive. Those on a tight budget should shop at the supermarket between the main square and the new part of town. There are many fish restaurants in the *barracas* on the beach.

### $$$ Cacau
*Quadrado 96, T073-3668 1296.*
The restaurant of choice for those who want to eat Bahian in Trancoso. The menu is strong on flavour and spices which includes starters like mini *acarajé* balls with *vatapá* or *caruru* and mains like *camarão nativo* (local prawns), served twitchingly fresh.

### $$$ Capim Santo
*R de Deco 55, Quadrado, T073 3668 1112, www.capimsanto.com.br.*
Paulistana ex-pat Sandra Marques' cooking is quintessentially Trancoso. Seafood dishes with a Bahian twist like prawn in manioc flour balls or tuna carpaccio are served under the stars by candlelight in a little tropical garden just off the Quadrado.

### $$$ Maritaca
*Quadrado, T073-3668 1258.*
A Marrakech theme may seem odd in hippy-chic Trancoso, but the sumptuous back deck at this new restaurant – with its open sky and beautiful drop-off view out to the sea – attracts a faithful cocktail crowd. The Italian food (with a big choice of pizzas) is adequate but lacks sparkle; slow service.

### $$ Cabana do Andrea
*Coqueiros Beach.*
The most fashionable place to sip and sun. Run by a Sardinian who serves great Italian wood-fired pizza, super-fresh ceviche and a gamut of fruity caipirinhas and tropical juices.

### $ Dona Maria
*On a tiny little tile stall on the Quadrado in front of the Ainarí boutique. Before 0900.*
This joyful old lady and her 9-year-old grandson sell delicious home-baked bread, tiny prawn, chicken *empadas* (meat pies) and steaming hot treacle-sweet black coffee to fishermen (or visiting surfers) who rise with the sun.

### $ Portinha
*Quadrado.*
Good-value pay-by-weight options and a wealth of juices.

## Espelho

### $$$ Silvinha's
*T073-9985 4157, sylviaespelho@yahoo.com.br.*
It's booking only if you want to eat under the thatch in this rustic chic restaurant set under coconut palms next to a clear-water stream behind the beach. But it's well worth it. Sylvinha's food is delicious, and dishes include freshly caught octopus accompanied by pureed plantain, peppered pineapple with mint and courgette in coconut and dendê sauce.

## Bars and clubs

### Arraial d'Ajuda
Porto Seguro does not have much in the way of nightlife; most visitors stay in Arraial across the water. In Arraial, the *lambada* is danced at the **Zouk** bar (in summer). Bars on the main streets have live music and dancing almost all year round. Many top Brazilian bands play at the beach clubs at **Praia do Parracho** in summer, entry is about US$10. Entry to other beach parties is about US$5.

## What to do

### Trancoso
Various tour operators around the main square sell *combi*, bus and air tickets for destinations throughout Bahia and organize day trips to Espelho and beyond.

**Mata N'ativa Travel**, *T073-8804 6830, www. matanativapousada.com.br*. Whale watching, boat trips to the southern beaches, wildlife visits to Estação Veracel, mountain biking, stand-up paddling and canoeing.
**Portomondo**, *Ponta do Apaga Fogo 1, Marina Quinta do Porto Hotel, T073-3668 1373, www.portomondo.com*. Tours from around Arraial, Trancoso, Caraíva and Corumbau to Jaqueira, Veracel, Monte Pascoal and Abrolhos. Excellent diving and ecotourism itineraries and car or helicopter transfers to hotels in Trancoso and further south.

### Caraíva

Boat trips (to Corumbau, Espelho and other destinations) and stand-up paddling on the river can be organized through the *pousadas* or through Ivan on the waterfront.

### Parque Nacional Marinho dos Abrolhos

If you are coming from Porto Seguro everything including transfers and accommodation in Caravelas can be arranged by **Pataxo** (page 82), **Portomondo** or **Mata N'ativa Travel** (see above). It is essential to book ahead as boats only sail when they have a minimum of 10 passengers. This is most likely in high season – when humpback whales visit the islands – between Jul and early Dec, when sightings are almost guaranteed.

From Caravelas, book with **Horizonte Aberto,** Av das Palmeiras 313, T073-3297 1474, horizonteaberto.com.br or **Catamarã Sanuk,** T073-3297 1344, T073-98871 6634, www.abrolhos.net. Both companies can organize multi-day live aboard dive trips.

## Transport

### Arraial d'Ajuda

It's not necessary to return to Porto Seguro to venture into the rest of Bahia. Arraial is connected by bus to **Eunápolis** and **Caraíva**, and **Trancoso** to the south. Various agencies in town offer transfers by buggy or Land Rover to **Corumbau** and beyond

all the way to **Abrolhos**. Pataxó (see page 82), **Portomondo** and **Mata N'ativa Travel** (see What to do, above) are the best and most reliable.

**Ferry** Take a bus or *combi* to the Rio Buranhém ferry dock, from where boats cross the river to **Porto Seguro**, on the north bank, 3-5 mins, US$0.60 for foot passengers, US$3 for cars, every 15-30 mins day and night. From there, it is a further 5 km to Arraial d'Ajuda town centre (US$1 by bus, *combis* charge US$0.85 per person, taxis US$3), although the first *pousadas* are literally on the Arraial riverbank.

### Trancoso

The easiest way to get around town is by bike, on foot or motorbike taxi.

**Air** Like any of the Bahian resorts, it is also possible to organize air taxis from Rio or São Paulo or helicopter transfers from Arraial, Caraíva and Corumbau; see **Pataxó** (page 82), **Portomondo** or **Mata N'ativa Travel** (see What to do, above) for details.

**Bus** In high season, *combis* ply the shorter dirt road along the coast between Arraial and Trancoso, leaving when full. Buses run along the smoother, paved road between Porto Seguro, Arraial d'Ajuda and Trancoso at least once an hour in high season (US$1.75 from Porto Seguro, US$1.25 from Arraial). Or catch the half-hourly boat across to **Porto Seguro** from the ferry port in Arraial in high season. Buses for **Caraíva** leave 2 times a day at 0800 and 1700, with an extra bus at 1200 in high season.

**Taxi** From Arraial a taxi costs around US$20; from Porto airport US$25-30.

### Caraíva

Caraíva is connected to **Trancoso** by 2 daily buses (3 in high season), along a very poor dirt road. The journey involves a river crossing and can take as long as 3 hrs in the wet season (Apr-Jun). Access roads are poor and almost impossible after heavy rain. **Aguia Azul** buses run to **Porto Seguro** twice daily (3 times in high season), along a very poor dirt road involving a river crossing. There is 1 additional daily service via Eunápolis. If heading south, take a bus to **Itabela** or **Eunápolis** (0600, 3 hrs), or take a taxi.

### Parque Nacional de Monte Pascoal
To **Caraíva** there is a river crossing by boats which are always on hand. There is 1 bus a day Mon-Fri to **Itamaraju**, 16 km to the south.

### Corumbau
Beach buggy taxis take you to the river crossing (US$30) to, or it's about a 12-km walk. The punt ferry across the river costs around US$3. Buses run to **Itmaraju** and beyond to **Curumuxatiba**.

### Caravelas
**Bus** Caravelas sits on the banks of the Rio Caravelas 36 km south of the larger town of **Prado** (on the BA-001) and around 20 km from **Teixeira de Freitas** on the BR-101 (both of which have better transport links). There are frequent buses to each town and Prado and Teixeira themselves have frequent buses to **Eunápolis** and **Itamaraju** from where there are connections to the rest of the state. There are 2 weekly buses to **Porto Seguro**, 4-5 hrs.

### Parque Nacional Marinho dos Abrolhos
The journey to the islands from Caravelas takes 3-4 hrs depending on sea conditions. Boats leave at 0700 or 0730 from the Marina Porto Abrolhos, some 5 km north of Caravelas town centre (around US$550 depending on numbers) and they return at dusk.

# Linha Verde &
## the northern coast

Heading north from Salvador airport, the BA-099 coast road, or Estrada de Coco (Coconut Highway), passes many coconut plantations and 50 km of beautiful beaches. From south to north the best known are Ipitanga (famous for its reefs), Buraquinho, Jauá, Arembepe, Guarajuba, Itacimirim, Castelo Garcia D'Ávila (where there is a 16th-century fort) and Forte. North of Praia do Forte, the road is called the 'Linha Verde' (Green Line), which runs for 142 km to the Sergipe state border. The road is more scenic than the BR-101, especially near Conde. There are very few hotels or *pousadas* in the more remote villages. Among the most picturesque are Subaúma and Baixio; the latter, where the Rio Inhambupe meets the sea, is very beautiful. Buses serve most of these destinations.

## Praia do Forte

smart mini-resort town with turtle nesting sites

Some 80 km north of Salvador, is a busy resort town much beloved of weekenders from Salvador. The fishing village that once lay at its heart is long gone and there are better beaches elsewhere in Bahia, but the resort is nonetheless one of the principal points of call for international visitors on a pre-booked trip.

Much of the area around the town is protected, with turtle-nesting beaches, remnant coastal *restinga* forest, and a small area of marshland, which is home to a large number of birds, caimans and capybara. Visits can be organized through the town's hotels and *pousadas*.

The town takes its name from the castle built by a Portuguese settler, Garcia D'Avila, in 1556, to warn Salvador of impending invasion by rival European powers. D'Avila was given a huge area of land, many times greater than the entire territory of his native Portugal and stretching from Praia do Forte deep into the northeast, on which he made the first farm in Brazil, cleared the virgin Atlantic forest, grazed by the first herd of cattle to the country and planted the first coconut and mango trees in Brazil.

**Projeto Tamar** ⓘ *Av Farol Garcia D'Ávila s/n, T071-3676 0321, www.tamar.org.br, daily 0830-1730, US$6.50*, have the largest visitor centre for the national turtle preservation programme in Brazil. This programme is by far – the most successful of its kind in the world, Visits are great for families. Come to see hatchlings, young turtles in the large tanks and for information on turtle preservation in Brazil, which has been so effective that Brazilian turtles are now swimming over reefs in the Caribbean and West Africa. Guides speak English.

## Listings Praia do Forte

### Where to stay

The town's main street had its name changed from Alameda do Sol to Av ACM, though it is often still referred to by the old name. In addition to the *pousadas* listed below, there are many package resorts and gated villa communities around the town.

#### $$$$ Aloha Brasil Pousada
*R da Aurora qd 21, lote 10, T071-3676 0279, www.pousadaalohabrasil.com.br.*
Well-appointed rooms in a large balcony-fronted building set in a tropical garden. Decent pool with sundecks. Generous breakfasts.

#### $$$$ Porto Zarpa Hotel
*R da Aurora, condominio Porto das Baleias, T071-3676 1414, www.portozarpa.com.br.*
Large 2-storey building overlooking a decent-sized pool and set in palm-shaded gardens, close to the beach, cable TV. Good for families.

#### $$$$ Tivoli Eco-Resort
*Av do Farol, T071-3676 4000, www.tivolihotels.com.*
A luxurious family resort owned by the high-end Tivoli group with a fabulous spa, large pool and boxy but beautfully-appointed rooms set in long annexes in tropical gardens by the beach at the entrance to town. Full programme of activities.

#### $$$ Sobrado da Vila
*Av ACM s/n, T071-3676 1088, www.sobradodavila.com.br.*
Nice boutique-style *pousada* with a small pool, wooden sun deck and colourful, cosy rooms with white tile flooring and rustic polished wood ceilings.

#### $$ Pousada João Sol
*R da Corvina 4, T071-3676 1054, www.pousadajoaosol.com.br.*
Chalets and apartments, with hammock-strung balconies in a low-key but well-appointed *pousada*. The owner speaks English, Spanish and German. Great breakfast.

#### $$ Pousada Tia Helena
*Just east of Praça dos Artistas, at Alameda das Estrelas, T071-3676 1198, T071-9901 2894 (mob), www. tiahelenapraiadoforte.com.br.*
Helena, the motherly proprietor, offers the best-value in town, with simple fan-cooled rooms, some large enough for families, and an enormous breakfast.

#### $ Albergue da Juventude
*Praia do Forte, R da Aurora 3, T071-3676 1094, www.albergue.com.br. Price per person.*
Smart youth hostel with decent shared rooms and rooms with en suites (**$$**), a large breakfast, fan, kitchen and shop, cheaper for HI members.

### Transport

**Bus** It is easy to flag down buses from the crossroads on the main highway out of town. To get there take a *combi* (every 15 mins, US$1) from town. Taxis are a rip-off. To **Salvador** buses run 5 times daily, 1 hr, US$4 (**Santa Maria/Catuense**). To **Estancia** in Sergipe, 4-5 daily, US$6.

Mangue Seco was immortalized in Jorge Amado's book *Tieta*. A steep hill rises behind the town to white-sand dunes that offer superb views of the coast. The encroaching dunes have caused the mangrove to dry up.

The long empty broad beach is spectacular and outside weekends almost completely empty but for a few fishermen. It's particularly wonderful under a full moon, when the white dunes and waves turn silvery and the reflected light is so bright it feels like twilight. Come for utter peace and tranquillity.

## Listings Mangue Seco

### Where to stay

There are plenty of small cheap places along the seafront from the jetty, none with addresses or phone numbers (the village is tiny). There are simple restaurants around the main square next to the church. The beach has a handful of *barracas* serving cheap fish.

#### $$ Fantasias do Agreste
*T075-3445 9011, www.pousadafantasias doagreste.com.br.*
Bright rooms with terraces overlooking a pool, decked out in tiled floors, whitewash and blocks of primary colour and furnished with wicker beds and light wood wardrobes.

#### $$ Village Mangue Seco
*T075-3224 2965, www.villagemangueseco. com.br.*
Mock-adobe concrete chalets (some a/c, some fan-cooled), sitting around a pool in a large palm-shaded lawn dotted with tropical flowers.

### Transport

The peninsula is connected to Pontal in the state of Sergipe by boat or canoe on the Rio Real (10-min crossing). Any Aracaju-bound bus will drop visitors at the town of **Estancia**, just across the border from Bahia in Sergipe state, from where there is 1 southbound bus a day to **Pontal** (a port comprising little more than a jetty, sitting opposite Mangue Seco) at 1500 and occasional Toyotas (leaving when full) from in front of the Estancia hospital. Alternatively, you can hire a taxi from Alex (T079-9600 3318). Infrequent slow boats cross the river from Pontal to Mangue Seco, usually 2-3 times daily. A private launch with Cesar (T079-9975 30590) will cost US$15, but there are invariably other people willing to share the boat and it is just a matter of waiting a while for them to turn up.

# Chapada Diamantina
## & the Sertão

The beautiful Chapada Diamantina National Park comprises a series of escarpments covered in *cerrado*, *caatinga* and moist tropical forest, dripping with waterfalls and studded with caves. Although little of the forest is original, there is still plenty of wildlife including jaguar and maned wolf, and the area is good for birdwatching. Various trails cut through the park offering walks from a few hours to a few days, and many leave from Lençóis, the ideal base for visiting the region.

The road from Salvador to Lençóis and the chapada passes through Feira de Santana, famous for its Micareta, an extremely popular out-of-season carnival. The harsh beauty of the *sertão* and its hospitable people are the reward for those wanting to get off the beaten track. The region has been scarred by droughts and a violent history of bandits, rebellions and religious leaders. Euclides da Cunha and Canudos are good places to start exploring this history. The Raso da Catarina, once a hiding place for Lampião, and the impressive Paulo Afonso waterfalls, can both be visited from the town of Paulo Afonso located on the banks of the São Francisco. This important river runs through the *sertão*, linking agricultural settlements such as Juazeiro, Ibotirama and Bom Jesus de Lapa and has its headwaters in northern Minas Gerais.

Lençóis (population 9000) is the best place from which to explore the *chapada*. It's a pretty little colonial village set on the banks of the fast-flowing Rio Lençóis, in the middle of the park. Many of the sights can be visited on foot from town. The streets of Lençóis are lined with rustic houses, many of which are now *pousadas*, restaurants or shops selling quirky handicrafts and semi-precious stones.

Lençóis was established as a mining town in 1844 and takes its name from the tents assembled by the prospectors who first arrived here (*lençóis* means 'white sheets' in Portuguese) set on the brown and green of the hillside. While there are still some *garimpeiros* (gold and diamond prospectors) left, tourism is now the main economic mainstay. Rather than precious metals, visitors are attracted by the cool climate and the wonderful trekking in the Diamantina hills. There is a tourist office, **Sectur**, inside the market next to the river.

### Around Lençóis
On walking trips from Lençóis it is possible to visit the *serrano* (in the hills above town), which has wonderful natural pools in the river bed that give a great spring-water massage when you sit under them; or the **Salão de Areia**, where the coloured sands for the bottle paintings come from.

## Lençóis

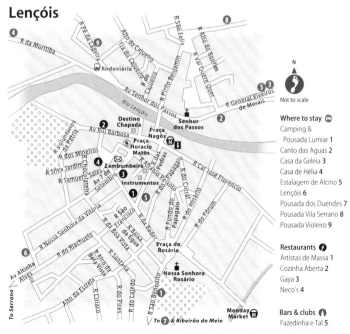

N
Not to scale

**Where to stay**
Camping &
  Pousada Lumiar 1
Canto das Aguas 2
Casa da Geleia 3
Casa de Hélia 4
Estalagem de Alcino 5
Lençóis 6
Pousada dos Duendes 7
Pousada Vila Serrano 8
Pousada Violeiro 9

**Restaurants**
Artistas de Massa 1
Cozinha Aberta 2
Gaya 3
Neco's 4

**Bars & clubs**
Fazedinha e Tal 5

Ribeirão do Meio is a 15-minute walk from town; here locals slide down a long natural water chute into a big pool (it is best to watch someone else first and take something to slide in).

Also near Lençóis are two very pretty waterfalls: the **Cachoeira da Primavera**; and the **Cachoeira Sossego**, a picture-postcard cascade plunging into a deep blue pool.

## Other towns in the Chapada

There is simple accommodation and a handful of tour operators in **Palmeiras**, some 55 km west of Lençóis. The town makes a far quieter alternative base for exploring the *chapada*. *Combis* run sporadically between Palmeiras and Lençóis.

**Mucugê** town in the far south, 134 km from Lençóis is sleepier still, and has a fascinating whitewash cemetery filled with elaborate mausoleums and set against the dark granite of the hillside. There are bus connections with Lençóis and Feira de Santana. The adjacent **Parque Municipal de Mucugê** was set up to protect the *sempre viva* or *chuveirinho* plant, a beautiful globe of white flowers whose popularity with flower arrangers in Brazil almost led to their extinction in the late 20th century.

**Igatu** has a population of approximately 350 people, some of them live in the largely abandoned stone houses built into or around Cyclopean boulders that dot the landscape. Wandering around the village and the ruins is a haunting experience. There are two *pousadas* in the village.

The **airport** ① *20 km from town, Km 209, BR-242, T075-3625 8100*, has twice weekly flights to and from Salvador, with **TRIP** ① *www.voetrip.com.br*. There are direct buses from Salvador and other cities in Bahia via Feira de Santana. Buses from Recife and the northeast come via Seabra, west of Lençóis.

## Listings Lençóis *map p101*

### Where to stay

#### $$$$ Canto das Águas
*Av Senhor dos Passos, T075-3334 1154, www.lencois.com.br.*
Medium-sized riverside hotel with modest a/c or fan-cooled rooms, a pool and efficient service. The best rooms are in the new wing; others can be musty.

#### $$$ Hotel de Lençóis
*R Altinha Alves 747, T075-3334 1102, www.hoteldelencois.com.br.*
Plain, dark wood and white-tiled rooms with terracotta roofs set in a handsome colonial house in a grassy garden on the edge of the park. Good breakfast, pool and a restaurant.

#### $$$ Pousada Vila Serrano
*R Alto do Bonfim 8, T075-3334 1486, www.vilaserrano.com.br.*
Warm and welcoming mock-colonial *pousada* overlooking a patio and little garden 5 mins from town. Excellent service, breakfast, trips organized. Very friendly and knowledgeable.

#### $$ Estalagem de Alcino
*R Gen Viveiros de Morais 139, T075-3334 1171, www.alcinoestalagem.com.*
An enchanting and beautifully restored period house with a range of rooms furnished with 19th-century antiques. Excellent breakfast.

#### $ Casa da Geleia
*R Gen Viveiros 187, T075-3334 1151, www.casadageleia.com.br.*
A handful of smart chalets set in a huge garden at the entrance to the town. English spoken, good breakfast, including sumptuous jams and honeys made or collected by the owner. Zé Carlos is a keen birdwatcher and an authority on the region.

### $ Casa de Hélia
*R da Muritiba, T075-3334 1143,*
*www.casadehelia.com.br.*
Attractive and welcoming little
guesthouse. English spoken.
Good facilities, legendary breakfast.

### $ HI Lençóis
*R Urbano Duarte 121, T075-3334 1497,*
*www.hostelchapada.com.br.*
A large, friendly and well-run hostel with
an adventure sports agency in one of the
town's grand old colonial houses. The
building has been completely restored
and has singles, en suite doubles and
single-sex 4- to 6-bed dorms; shared
kitchen and a large, airy garden with
hammocks and littered with outdoor chairs.

### $ Pousada dos Duendes
*R do Pires, T075-3334 1229,*
*www.pousadadosduendes.com.*
Run by English Olivia Taylor and often
crowded with backpackers. Rooms are basic
with shared showers, modest breakfast
and dinner (with veggie options). Their tour
agency, **H2O Expeditions**, arranges tours
and treks from 1 to 11 days. Check with other
agencies in town before committing.

### $ Pousada Violeiro
*R Prof Assis 70, T075-3334 1259,*
*www.pousadavioleiro.com.br.*
Very simple rooms with room for up to
4 just behind the bus stop near the river.
Quiet and conservative.

### Camping

### Camping and Pousada Lumiar
*Near the Rosário church in the town centre,*
*T075-9984 1300, www.pousadaecamping*
*lumiar.com.br.*
A large grassy area for pitching tents and a
series of very simple rooms and bungalows.
Popular restaurant. Friendly.

## Restaurants

### $$$ Cozinha Aberta
*Rui Barbosa 42, just east of the main praça,*
*T075-3334 1309, www.cozinhaaberta.com.br.*
The best in town with organic and slow food
from Paulistana chef Deborah Doitschinoff.

### $$ Artistas da Massa
*R Miguel Calmon 49, T075-3334 1886.*
Italian dishes, mainly pasta and pizza.

### $$ Neco's Bar
*Praça Maestro Clarindo Pachêco 15,*
*T075-3334 1179.*
Set meal of local dishes of the kind once
eaten by the *garimpeiro* miners, such as
saffron-stewed mutton accompanied by
prickly pear cactus, crisp, tart *batata da terra*
and fried green banana.

## Shopping

There is a little market in the main square
selling arts and crafts and shops in the town
selling Bahian musical instruments and
ceramic figurines.

## What to do

### Birdwatching
**Ciro Albano**, *www.nebrazilbirding.com.*
The best birding guide for the northeast of
Brazil offering tips to birding and wildlife
sites, including Estação Veracruz, Canudos
and the Chapada Diamantina.

### Guides
Guides offer their services at most *pousadas*
(about US$20-30 per trip); most of them are
very young. The following are recommended:
**Chapada Adventure**, *Av 7 de Setembro 7,*
*T075-3334 2037, www.chapadaadventure.*
*com.br.* A small operator offering good-value
car-based tours and light hiking throughout
the *chapada.*
**Edmilson** (known as **Mil**), *R Domingos B*
*Souza 70, T075-3334 1319.* Knowledgeable
and reliable guide who knows the region
extremely well.

**Fora da Trilha**, *R das Pedras 202, www. foradatrilha.com.br*. Longer hikes and light adventures, from canyoning to rapelling.
**Luiz Krug**, *contact via Vila Serrano, T075-3334 1102*. An independent, English-speaking guide specializing in geology and caving.
**Venturas**, *R da Baderna, T075-99979 5115 9494, www.venturas.com.br*. Excellent trekking expeditions, up to 6 days.
**Zé Carlos**, *contact through Casa da Geleia or Vila Serrano*. The best guide for birdwatching.

## Transport

**Air** Airport, Km 209, BR-242, 20 km from town T075-3625 8100. Twice weekly flights from **Salvador** with **TRIP** (www.voetrip.com.br).

**Bus** Real Expresso to **Salvador** 3 a day, US$25, *comercial* via Feira de Santana. Book in advance, especially at weekends and holidays. For the rest of Bahia state change at Feira de Santana; it is not necessary to go via Salvador. Buses also to **Recife**, **Ibotirama**, **Barreiras** or **Palmas** (for Jalapão), **Chapada dos Veadeiros** and **Brasília**, 16 hrs, US$65 (all with transfer in Seabra, several buses daily).

## Parque Nacional da Chapada Diamantina

one of the highlights of inland Bahia

The Chapada Diamantina National Park was founded in 1985 and comprises 1500 sq km of escarpment broken by extensive tracts of *caatinga* scrub forest, *cerrado*, patches of moist Atlantic coast forest and *pântano* (wetlands with permanent plant growth). The diverse ecosystems have an associated diversity of flora and fauna. There is very little primary forest left, but the area is nonetheless home to rare large mammals such as maned wolf, jaguar and ocelot and birds endemic to all of the ecosystems. Spectaculars include the king vulture, crowned eagle, red-legged seriema and blue-winged macaw. There are birding guides available in Lençóis (see What to do, above).

The **park headquarters** ⓘ *R Barão do Rio Branco 25, Palmeiras, T075-3332 2420*, is 50 km from Lençóis. However, Lençóis is a much more practical source of information and the numerous agencies make it easy to find out what's what. See also www.infochapada.com.

Roy Funch, an American who used to manage the park and who now offers guided walks, has written an excellent book on the *chapada*: A Visitor's Guide to the Chapada Diamantina Mountains (Collection Apoio 45), in English and Portuguese. The book includes history and geology of the region, an itinerary of all the principal sights, with instructions on how to reach them and a thorough, though not comprehensive, checklist of birds and mammals. It is widely available in Lençóis.

### Visiting the park
The *chapada* is cut by dirt roads, trails and rivers, which lead to waterfalls, viewpoints on table-top mountains, caves and natural swimming holes. There are many different hikes, and many of the routes have been used for centuries by the local farmers and miners.

There are over 20 tour operators in Lençóis and organizing a trip to even the most distant sights is straightforward. Most tours tend to be car-based and rather sedentary as these are more profitable. But there are plenty of great hikes and sights

**Tip...**
Finding your own way along the hiking routes is difficult and it is best to visit the park on a guided trip.

around Lençóis, so consider all the options before signing up. Brazilian tourists are often more interested in chatting loudly among themselves than in hearing the quiet music of nature, so it can be difficult to see wildlife. See What to do, page 103.

The most impressive sights in the *chapada* are included in the standard packages; most have an entrance fee. Trips include the extensive **Gruta do Lapa Doce** (US$3) and Pratinha caves (US$3); the latter are cut

## Chapada Diamantina

through to glassy blue water. The table-top mountains at the **Morro de Pai Inácio**, US$1.25, 30 km from Lençóis, offer the best view of the *chapada*, especially at sunset. The 384-m-high **Cachoeira da Fumaça** (Smoke or Glass Waterfall) is the second highest in Brazil and lies deeper within the park 2½ hours hike from the village of **Capão**. The view is astonishing; the updraft of the air currents often makes the water flow back up creating the 'smoke' effect. The **Rio Marimbus** flows through and area of semi-swamp reminiscent of the Pantanal and is very rich in birdlife; whilst the **Rio Mucugezinho** plunges over the blood-red **Cachoeira do Diabo** in an extensive area of *cerrado* just below the craggy **Roncador** ('snorer') waterfall.

### Hiking in the chapada

It is essential to use a guide for treks as it is easy to get lost. Trail-walking in the park can involve clambering over rocks and stepping stones so bring strong shoes. A reasonable level of physical fitness is advisable. There are a lot of mosquitos in campsites so carry repellent. For overnight trips it is highly advisable to bring a fleece and sleeping bag as nights in the 'winter' months can be cold. Sometimes, guides can arrange these. A tent is useful but optional; although many camps are beside reasonably hospitable caves. Torches (flashlights) and a water bottle are essentials.

The **Morro do Pai Inacio to Capão** trail is a 25-km day hike that leads from the summit of the Pai Inácio escarpment around other table-top mountains, passing through *cerrado*, *caatinga* and arable areas to the Capão Valley. Another day hike is from **Lençóis to Capão**, along a series of rivers (great for swimming) and around the base of the mountains, with a car ride back at the end of the walk.

## Parque Nacional da Chapada Diamantina

The *chapada* forms part of the Brazilian shield, one of the oldest geological formations on earth, dating from the when the world was only one land mass. It extends north into the Serra da Capivara and Jalapão, and south into the Serra do Espinhaço and Serra da Canastra in Minas and the mountains of Mato Grosso and northern Bolivia.

Cave paintings and petroglyphs suggest that people have been living in and around the *chapada* for millennia. However, there were no permanent settlers in the hills in recorded history until the arrival of Portuguese prospectors in the 1700s, who discovered gold and diamonds in the extreme south of the *chapada* near Livramento de Nossa Senhora and in the north near Jacobina. The Portuguese kept the findings secret for fear of driving down world gem prices, and ceding the *chapada* to other European powers, notably the Dutch and Spanish, who were invading and occupying Brazilian territory repeatedly during this period.

The *chapada* didn't open up fully to mining until 1844, when Mucugê, Rio de Contas and subsequently Lençóis were founded and settled by miners from neighbouring Minas Gerais and western Bahia, followed by Portuguese noblemen from the Bahian coast. The latter evolved into *coroneis*: robber barons who set up ruthless local fiefdoms run by gun-toting *jangada* henchmen. The most famous was Horácio de Mattos, a prototype for many modern-day rural Brazilian politicians. De Mattos sucked all the money out of the *chapada* with his personal campaigns. He carried out famous vendettas against two other *coroneis*, Manuel Fabrício de Oliveira and Militão Rodrigues Coelho, to establish patriarchal dominance, overthrew the state government, routed the federal army and chased the infamous communist Prestes column all the way across Brazil and into Bolivia. He was arrested in Salvador in 1930 and assassinated in mysterious circumstances the following year.

The **Cachoeira da Fumaça** trail leaves direct from Lençóis and takes two to three days to reach the base of the falls, from where there is a steep hike to the top. If you only have one day, it's possible to drive the 70 km to the **Vale do Capão** and hike the steep 6-km trail to the top of the falls. Both trails are very popular in high season.

A trail runs from **Igatu to Andaraí**, leaving from the central square of the former town past the cemetery and following the Xique-Xique River. The walk takes four hours and offers wonderful views of the mountain landscape. There are plenty of river bank stops for a cooling swim. There are longer treks too.

The **Vale do Paty** hike is a four- to six-day walk running through the heart of the *serra* along a valley surrounded by imposing *meseta* table-top mountains. There are many good stopping places with viewpoints, caves, swimming holes and waterfalls. The route usually departs from Capão in the north or from the village of Guiné just west of Andaraí town.

For a full cross-section of the park, hike the 112-km **Travessia Diamantina**, which runs from the Vale do Capão in the north right across the park via the Vale do Paty, to the Cachoeira do Buracão in the far south. Accommodation is in tents and rustic *pousadas* and there are side trips off to the Cachoeira da Fumaça (near Capão), Igatu, Poço Encatado, and the Marimbus Pantanal area and Roncador falls. Establish which of the sights you would like to visit with the tour company before setting off.

a rarely visited backland that has produced some of Brazil's most enduring mythical figures

Most of Bahia is arid: a rock and scrub semi-desert covered in leafless *caatinga* forest, cut by the blue vein of the majestic Rio São Francisco and dotted with little settlements where local people scratch a meagre living from the sun-baked earth. Tourists are seldom seen and are always a curiosity.

This is the *sertão* – famous for **Antônio Conselheiro**, a purple-robed desert prophet whose rag-tag band of marauders and bandits converted to Christianity in the late 19th-century and built Canudos, crushed two armies and almost broke the Brazilian state. **Lampião** – the *sertão*'s brutal Robin Hood – pillaged the rich *coroneis*, distributed wealth and brutal justice to the desert villages in the early 20th century and died in a gun battle in a town famous for its troubadours and poets. Their legacy, the iron hand of *coroneis* who impose rough justice to this day, and countless forgotten, timeless festivals and rites still characterize the dust and dirt towns of this vast interior.

The story of Conselheiro and the Canudos war was vividly depicted in Euclides da Cunha's *Os Sertões* (*Rebellion in the Backlands*). See also Mario Vargas Llosa's superb modern re-telling, *The War of the End of the World*.

### Euclides da Cunha and Monte Santo

North of Feira da Santana, at Km 225 on the BR-116 road to Fortaleza, **Euclides da Cunha**, is a good base for exploring the Canudos area with a couple of standard hotels. The *rodoviária* is on the BR-116, T075-3271 1365.

About 38 km west is the famous hill shrine of **Monte Santo** in the *sertão*, reached by 3.5 km of steps cut into the rocks of the **Serra do Picaraça**. It's a 45-minute walk each way, so set off early. This is the scene of pilgrimages and great religious devotion during **Holy Week**. The shrine was built by an Italian who had a vision of the cross on the mountain in 1765. One block north of the bottom of the stairs is the **Museu do Sertão**, with pictures from the 1897 Canudos rebellion.

### Canudos

Canudos itself is 100 km away. Religious rebels, led by Antônio Conselheiro, defeated three expeditions sent against them in 1897 before being overwhelmed. The Rio Vaza Barris, which runs through Canudos, has been dammed, and the town has been moved to **Nova Canudos** by the dam. Part of the old town is still located 10 km west in the **Parque Estadual de Canudos**, created in 1997.

The 1500-ha **Estação Biológica de Canudos** lies a few kilometres from the state park. It was founded in 1989 by the **Fundação Biodiversitas** ① *www.biodiversitas.org.br*, to protect the only remaining nesting sites of the critically endangered giant blue Lear's macaw. Fewer than 100 birds nest here, on a large sun-baked clay cliff within the reserve. The park and reserve can only be visited with a hire car, or by taxi from Canudos town. The Estação Biológica de Canudos can also be visited on a birding tour with guides such as **Ciro Albano** (see page 84). There are direct buses to Canudos from Salvador. For tourist information see www.canudosnet.com.br.

## Where to stay

### Euclides da Cunha and Monte Santo

**$$ Mirante**
*R Isaías Ferreira Canário 15,*
*Euclides da Cunha, T075-3271 1203,*
*www.hotelmirante-bahia.com.br.*
Standard town hotel with breakfast in the price.

### Canudos

**$ Marcell**
*R Ademar de Bastos, T075-3494 2015.*
Plain, simple rooms with or without a/c. In a
quiet suburb with views out over Canudos.

## Transport

### Canudos

At least 4 buses daily leave Salvador's
*rodoviária* for the city of **Euclides da Cunha**.
From here there are regular connections to
Canudos. Taxis in Canudos town can be hired
for a full day for around US$40.

# Practicalities

# **Getting** there

International flights arrive at at **Luís Eduardo Magalhães Airport** ⓘ *28 km east of the centre of Salvador, Praça Gago Coutinho, São Cristóvão, T071-3204 1010, www.aeroporto salvador.net* (see page 27). The airport in Porto Seguro, **Aeroporto de Porto Seguro** ⓘ *Estrada do Aeroporto s/n, 2 km north of town, T073-3288 1880*, in southern Bahia, has excellent connections to Rio de Janeiro, Belo Horizonte and São Paulo, so there is no reason to fly to southern Bahia via Salvador.

Prices are cheapest in October, November and after Carnaval and at their highest in the European summer and the Brazilian high seasons (generally 15 December to 15 January,

## TRAVEL TIP
## Packing for Brazil

**Bag** Unobtrusive sturdy bag (either rucksack or bag with wheels) and an inelegant day pack/bag – to attract minimal attention on the streets.

**Clothing** Brazilians dress casually. It's best to do likewise and blend in. Avoid flashy brands. Thin cotton or a modern wicking artificial fabric are best. Take lightweight trousers, shorts, a long-sleeved shirt, skirts, cotton or wicking socks, underwear, shawl or light waterproof jacket for evenings and a sun hat.

**Footwear** Light Gore-Tex walking shoes (or boots if you intend to trek) are best. Buy from a serious, designated outdoor company like Brasher or Berghaus rather than a flimsy fashion brand. Wear them in before you come. Nothing gives a tourist away more than new shoes.

**Sponge bag** 2% tincture of iodine; Mercurochrome or similar; athlete's foot powder; tea tree oil; antibiotic ointment; toothbrush; rehydration tablets; anti-diarrheals such as Imodium; sun protection (high factor) – this is expensive in Brazil.

**Electronics** UK, US or European socket adaptor; camera with case to attract minimal attention; torch (flashlight).

**Miscellaneous items** Ear plugs for surfing, traffic noise and cockerels at dawn; pen knife; strong string (3 m); hooks with a screw-in thread (for mosquito net); gaffer tape; sunglasses (with UV filter); money belt; a sealable waterproof bag large enough for camera and clothes.

For rural and beach destinations take a mosquito net impregnated with insect repellent (the bell-shaped models are best) and a water bottle.

### What not to pack – to buy there
T-shirts (local brands make you less conspicuous and they are sold everywhere); insect repellent (Johnson's Off! aerosol is best); beachwear (unless you have neuroses about your body – no one cares if their bum looks big in anything in Brazil); flip-flops (Havaianas); painkillers; shampoo and soap; toothpaste; beach sarong (*kanga*); vitamins; hammock and rope.

the Thursday before Carnaval to the Saturday after Carnaval, and 15 June to 15 August). Departure tax is usually included in the cost of the ticket.

The best deals on flights within Brazil are available through **Azul** ⓘ *www.voeazul. com.br*; **GOL** ⓘ *www.voegol.com.br*; and **TAM** ⓘ *www.tam.com.br*; and **Avianca** ⓘ *www. avianca.com.br*.

## Air passes

TAM and GOL offer a 21-day **Brazil Airpass**, which is valid on any TAM destination within Brazil and which includes both Salvador and Port Seguro. The price varies according to the number of flights taken and the international airline used to arrive in Brazil. They can only be bought outside Brazil. Rates vary depending on the season. Children pay a discounted rate; those under three pay 10% of the adult rate. Some of the carriers operate a blackout period between 15 December and 15 January.

## Baggage allowance

Airlines will only allow a certain weight of luggage without a surcharge; for Brazil this is usually two items of 32 kg but may be as low as 20 kg for domestic flights; with two items of hand luggage weighing up to 10 kg in total. UK airport staff can refuse to load bags weighing more than 30 kg. Baggage allowances are higher in business and first class. In all cases it is best to enquire beforehand.

## Sea

Travelling as a passenger on a cargo ship to South America is not a cheap way to go, but if you have the time and want a bit of luxury, it makes a great alternative to flying. The passage is often only available for round trips and generally calls at Rio de Janeiro only, though some ships sail to Salvador.

### Shipping agents

**Cargo Ship Voyages Ltd** ⓘ *Hemley, Woodbridge, Suffolk IP12 4QF, T01473-736265, www.cargoshipvoyages.co.uk*. Other companies include **Freighter Expeditions** ⓘ *www. freighterexpeditions.com.au*, and **Stradn** ⓘ *www.strandtravelltd.co.uk*.

### Cruise ships

Cruise ships regularly visit Brazil. The website www.cruisetransatlantic.com has full details of transatlantic crossings. There are often cheaper deals off season.

# **Getting** around

First time visitors seldom realise how big Brazil is and fail to plan accordingly. The country is the world's fifth largest, making it bigger than the USA without Alaska, or the size of Australia with France and the UK tagged on. Bahia itself is a little larger than Spain. As intercity rail is non-existent (but for one irregular and inconsequential route outside Bahia), travelling overland can involve long bus or car journeys.

## Air

Due to the huge distances between places, flying is the most practical option to get around. All state capitals and larger cities are linked with each other with services several times a day, and all national airlines offer excellent service, and reaching Porto Seguro in southern Bahia from Rio or other cities in the southeast of Brazil connected with Europe or the USA is as easy as reaching that city from Salvador. Deregulation of the airlines has greatly reduced prices on some routes and low-cost airlines offer fares that can often be as cheap as travelling by bus (when booked online). Buy your internal flights before leaving home. Paying with an international credit card is not always possible online within Brazil (as sites often ask for a Brazilian social security number), but it is usually possible to buy an online ticket through a hotel, agency or willing friend without a surcharge. Many smaller airlines go in and out of business sporadically. **Avianca** ⓘ *www.avianca.com.br*, **Azul** ⓘ *www.voeazul.com.br*, **GOL** ⓘ *www.voegol.com.br*, **TAM** ⓘ *www.tam.com.br*, and **TRIP** ⓘ *www.voetrip.com.br*, operate the most extensive routes.

## Road

### Bus

Other than flying, the most reliable way of travelling is by bus. Routes are extensive, prices reasonable and buses modern and comfortable. There are three standards of intercity and interstate bus: *Comum*, or *Convencional*, are quite slow, not very comfortable and fill up quickly; *Executivo* are more expensive, comfortable (many have reclining seats), and don't stop en route to pick up passengers so are safer; *leito* (literally 'bed') run at night between the main centres, offering reclining seats with leg rests, toilets, and sometimes refreshments, at double the normal fare. For journeys over 100 km, most buses have chemical toilets (bring toilet paper). Air conditioning can make buses cold at night, so take a jumper; on some services blankets are supplied.

Buses stop fairly frequently (every two to four hours) at *postos* for snacks. Bus stations for long-distance routes are called *rodoviárias*. They are frequently outside the city centres and offer snack bars, lavatories, left luggage, local bus services and information centres. Buy bus tickets at *rodoviárias* (most now take credit cards), not from travel agents who add on surcharges. Reliable bus information is hard to come by, other than from companies themselves. Buses usually arrive and depart in very good time. Many town buses have turnstiles, which can be inconvenient if you are carrying a large pack. Urban buses normally serve local airports.

### Car hire

Car hire is competitive with mainland Europe and a little pricier than the USA. But roads are not always well-signposted and maps are hard to come by. Use a sat nav only outside the cities. Within a city a sat nav offers the shortest routes, which can involve potentially dangerous crossings through peripheral communities. Costs can be reduced by reserving a car over the internet through one of the larger international companies such as **Europcar** ⓘ *www.europcar.co.uk*, or **Avis** ⓘ *www.avis.co.uk*. The minimum age for renting a car is 21 and it's essential to have a credit card. Companies operate under the terms *aluguel de automóveis* or *auto-locadores*. Check exactly what the company's insurance policy covers. In many cases it will not cover major accidents or 'natural' damage (eg flooding). Ask if extra cover is available. Sometimes using a credit card automatically includes insurance. Beware of being billed for scratches that were on the vehicle before you hired it. Avoid driving at night, especially away from the Bahian coast,

## Taxi

At the outset, make sure the meter is cleared and shows 'tariff 1', except (usually) from 2300-0600, Sunday, and in December when '2' is permitted. Check that the meter is working; if not, fix the price in advance. The **radio taxi** service costs about 50% more but cheating is less likely. Taxis outside larger hotels usually cost more. If you are seriously cheated, note the number of the taxi and insist on a signed bill; threatening to take it to the police can work. **Mototaxis** are much more economical, but many are unlicensed and there have been a number of robberies of passengers. Taxis vary widely in quality and price but are easy to come by and safe when taken from a *posto de taxis* (taxi rank).

# Essentials A-Z

## Accident and emergency

**Ambulance** T192. **Police** T190/197. If robbed or attacked, contact the tourist police. If you need to claim on insurance, make sure you get a police report.

## Children

Travel with children is easy in Brazil. Bahians love children and they are generally welcome everywhere. Facilities are often better than those back home. Most restaurants provide children's seats and menus as well as crayons and paper to keep them happy. Children are never expected to be seen but not heard. Children under 3 generally travel for 10% on internal flights and at 70% until 12 years old. Prices on buses depend on whether the child will occupy a seat or a lap. Laps are free and if there are spare seats after the bus has departed the child can sit there for free. On tours children under 6 usually go free or it may be possible to get a discount.

Some hotels charge a cheaper family rate. Some will not charge for children under 5 and most can provide an extra camp bed for a double room. A few of the more romantic boutique beach resorts around Trancoso and Itacaré do not accept children. If you are planning to stay in such a hotel it is best to enquire ahead.

## Disabled travellers

As in most Latin American countries, facilities are generally very poor. Problems are worst for **wheelchair users**, who will find that ramps are rare and that toilets and bathrooms with facilities are few and far between, except for some of the more modern hotels and the larger airports. Public transport is not well geared up for wheelchairs and pavements are often in a poor state of repair or crowded with street vendors requiring passers-by to brave the traffic. The metro has lifts and disabled chair lifts at some stations (but not all are operational). Disabled Brazilians obviously have to cope with these problems and mainly rely on the help of others to get on and off public transport and generally move around. Drivers should bring a disabled sticker as most shopping centres and public car parks have disabled spaces.

**Disability Travel**, www.disabilitytravel.com, is an excellent US site written by travellers in wheelchairs who have been researching disabled travel full-time since 1985. There are many tips and useful contacts and articles and the company also organizes group tours.
**Global Access – Disabled Travel Network Site**, www.globalaccessnews.com. Provides travel information for 'disabled adventurers' and includes a number of reviews and tips.
**Society for Accessible Travel and Hospitality**, www.sath.org. Has some specific information on Brazil.

Brazilian organizations include: **Sociedade Amigos do Deficiente Físico**, T021-2241 0063, based in Rio and with associate memberships throughout Brazil; and **Centro da Vida Independente**, Rio, www.cvi-rio. org.br. There are a number of specialist and general operators offering holidays specifically aimed at those with disabilities. These include: **Responsible Travel**, www.responsibletravel.com; **CanbeDone**, www.canbedone.co.uk; and **Access Travel**, www.access-travel.co.uk.

*Nothing Ventured*, edited by Alison Walsh (Harper Collins), has personal accounts of worldwide journeys by disabled travellers, plus advice and listings.

## TRAVEL TIP
### Brazilian etiquette

In his 1941 travel book, *I Like Brazil*, Jack Harding said of Brazilians that "anyone who does not get along with (them) had better examine himself; the fault is his." And perhaps the best writer on Brazil in English, Joseph Page, observed in his 1995 book *The Brazilians* that "cordiality is a defining characteristic of their behaviour. They radiate an irresistible pleasantness, abundant hospitality, and unfailing politeness, especially to foreigners." It is hard to offend Brazilians or to find Brazilians offensive, but to make sure you avoid misunderstandings, here are a few, perhaps surprising, tips.

**Public nudity**, even toplessness on beaches, is an arrestable offence.

**Brazilians will talk to anyone, anywhere.** "Sorry, do I know you?" is the least Brazilian sentiment imaginable and no one ever rustles a newspaper on the metro.

**Walks in nature are never conducted in silence.** This has led many Brazilians to be unaware that their country is the richest in terrestrial wildlife on the planet.

**Drug use**, even of marijuana, is deeply frowned upon. Attitudes are far more conservative than in Europe. The same is true of public drunkenness.

**When driving** it is normal, especially in Rio, to accelerate right up the bumper of the car in the lane in front of you on the highway, hoot repeatedly and flash your headlights. It is considered about as rude as ringing the doorbell in Brazil.

**The phrase 'So para Ingles Ver'** ('just for the English to see') is a common expression that means 'to appear to do something by the rule book whilst doing the opposite'.

**This is the land of red tape.** You need a social security number to buy a SIM card and fingerprint ID just to go to the dentist.

**Never presume a policeman will take a bribe.** And never presume he won't. Let the policeman do the presuming.

**Never insult an official.** You could find yourself in serious trouble.

**Brazilians are very private** about their negative emotions. Never moan for more than a few seconds, even with justification – you will be branded an *uruca* (harbinger of doom), and won't be invited to the party.

**Never confuse a Brazilian footballer** with an Argentine one.

**Brazilians believe that anyone can dance samba.** They can't.

**Never dismiss a street seller** with anything less than cordiality; an impolite dismissal will be seen as arrogant and aggressive. Always extend a polite "não obrigado".

**Brazilian time.** Peter Fleming, the author of one of the best travel books about Brazil, once said that "a man in a hurry will be miserable in Brazil." Remember this when you arrive 10 minutes late to meet a friend in a bar and spend the next hour wondering if they've already gone after growing tired of waiting for you. They haven't. They've not yet left home. Unless you specify 'a hora britanica' then you will wait. And wait. And everyone will be mortified if you complain.

## Electricity

Generally 110 V 60 cycles AC, but occasionally 220 V 60 cycles AC is used. European and US 2-pin plugs and sockets.

## Embassies and consulates

For a list of Brazilian embassies abroad, see http://embassygoabroad.com.

## Gay and lesbian travellers

Metropolitan Brazil is a good country for gay and lesbian travellers as attitudes are fairly liberal. Opinions in rural areas, however, are far more conservative and it is wise to adapt to this.

Festivals include the nationwide **Mix Brasil festival of Sexual diversity**, www.mixbrasil.uol.com.br.

## Health

See your GP or travel clinic at least 6 weeks before departure for general advice on travel risks and vaccinations. Make sure you have sufficient medical travel insurance, get a dental check, know your own blood group and, if you suffer a long-term condition such as diabetes or epilepsy, obtain a **Medic Alert** bracelet (www.medicalalert.co.uk).

### Vaccinations and anti-malarials

Confirm that your primary courses and boosters are up to date. It is advisable to vaccinate against polio, tetanus, typhoid, hepatitis A and, for more remote areas, rabies. Yellow fever vaccination is obligatory for most areas. Cholera, diphtheria and hepatitis B vaccinations are sometimes advised. Only a very few parts of Brazil have significant malaria risk and there has been no malaria recorded in Bahia for many years. It is however best to seek specialist advice before you leave.

## Health risks

The major risks posed in the region are those caused by insect disease carriers such as mosquitoes and sandflies. The key parasitic and viral diseases are South American trypanosomiasis (Chagas disease) and dengue fever. **Dengue fever** (which is present throughout Brazil) is particularly hard to protect against as the mosquitoes can bite throughout the day as well as night (unlike those that carry malaria; see box, page 118, for advice on avoiding insect bites. **Chagas disease** is spread by faeces of the triatomine, or assassin bugs, whereas sandflies spread a disease of the skin called **leishmaniasis**.

While standards of hygiene in Brazilian restaurants are generally very high, **intestinal upsets** are common, if only because many first time visitors are not used to the food. Always wash your hands before eating and be careful with drinking water and ice; if you have any doubts about the water then boil it or filter and treat it. In a restaurant buy bottled water or ask where the water has come from. Food can also pose a problem, be wary of salads if you don't know if it has been washed or not.

There is some risk of **tuberculosis** (TB) and although the BCG vaccine is available, it is still not guaranteed protection. It is best to avoid unpasteurized dairy products and try not to let people cough and splutter all over you.

Zika virus is present in Bahia but is less of a risk than dengue.. It is recommended that you check with the Foreign Office (www.gov.uk) before travelling, particularly if you're pregnant or planning to become pregnant, and seek advice from a health professional.

### Websites

**www.cdc.gov** Centres for Disease Control and Prevention (USA).
**www.fitfortravel. nhs.uk** Fit for Travel (UK), A-Z of vaccine and travel health advice for each country.

## TRAVEL TIP

### How to avoid insect bites

Brazilian insects are vectors for a number of diseases including zika, chikungunya, dengue and, in some areas, malaria and yellow fever. These are transmitted by mosquitoes (and some by sandflies) which bite both day and night. Here are a few tips to avoid getting bitten.

- Be particularly vigilant around dawn and dusk when most diurnal and nocturnal mosquitoes bite. Cover ankles and feet and the backs of arms.
- Check your room for insects and spray insecticide before you go out for the day to ensure an insect-free night. Most hotels will have spray, otherwise it can be bought in pharmacies and supermarkets.
- Use insect repellent, especially in beach and forested areas. No repellent works 100%, but most will limit bites. Repellent is available at most pharmacies and supermarkets throughout Brazil. The Off! brand is reliable. If you wish to make your own 'industrial-chemical-free' formula, the author finds the following recipe made with essential oils effective throughout Brazil, including the Amazon: 70% jojoba oil, 30% citronella oil, 10-20 drops of Eucalyptus radiata, 10-15 drops of Wintergreen, 10-15 drops of Cajeput. Do not take this formula internally. This insect repellent also works with sandflies who cannot land on the thick jojoba oil.
- Sandflies are not as widely present in Brazil as in Central America but you will encounter them in some locations (most notably Ilhabela). Many DEET repellents and citronella-based repellents do not work on sandflies. The recipe above, jojoba oil or 'Skin so Soft' baby oil does but you need to apply it thickly.
- Bring a mosquito net. Bell nets are best. Lifesystems do treated models which repel and kill insects. Bring a small roll of duct tape, a few screw-in hooks and at least 5 m of string to ensure you can put the net up in almost all locations.
- Sleep with the fan on when you sleep. Fans are for stopping mosquitoes as much as they are for cooling.
- Consider using insect-repellent treated shirts like those in the Craghoppers Nosilife range. Avoid black clothing. Mosquitoes find it attractive.

**www.fco.gov.uk** Foreign and Commonwealth Office (FCO), UK.
**www.itg.be** Prince Leopold Institute for Tropical Medicine.
**http://travelhealthpro.org.uk** Useful website for the National Travel Health Network and Centre (NaTHNaC), a UK government organization.
**www.who.int** World Health Organization.

### Books

Dawood, R, editor, *Travellers' health*, Oxford University Press, 2012.
Warrell, David, and Sarah Anderson, editors, *Oxford Handbook of Expedition and Wilderness Medicine*, Oxford Medical Handbooks2008.
Wilson-Howarth, Jane. *The Essential Guide to Travel Health*, Cadogan 2009.

## Insurance

Always take out travel insurance before you set off and read the small print carefully. Check that the policy covers the activities you intend or may end up doing. Also check exactly what your medical cover includes (eg ambulance, helicopter rescue or emergency flights back home). Also check the payment protocol. You may have to cough up first before the insurance company reimburses you. To be safe, it is always best to dig out all the receipts for expensive personal effects like jewellery or cameras. Take photos of these items and note down all serial numbers.

## Internet

Internet usage is widespread. Most hotels offer in-room Wi-Fi (usually free but sometimes at exorbitant rates).

## Language *See also page 129.*

Brazilians speak Portuguese, and very few speak anything else. Spanish may help you to be understood a little, but spoken Portuguese will remain undecipherable even to fluent Spanish speakers. To get the best out of Brazil, learn some Portuguese before arriving. Brazilians are the best thing about the country and without Portuguese you will not be able to interact beyond stereotypes and second guesses. Language classes are available in the larger cities and schools are listed in the What to do sections in this book.

Cactus (www.cactuslanguage.com), **Languages abroad** (www.languagesabroad. co.uk) and **Travellers Worldwide** (www. travellersworld wide.com) are among the companies that can organize language courses in Brazil. **McGraw Hill** and **DK** (*Hugo Portuguese in Three Months*) offer the best teach-yourself books. **Sonia Portuguese** (www.sonia-portuguese.com) is a useful online resource and there are myriad free and paid-for Portuguese apps of varying quality. Salvador is a popular place to learn Portuguese and there are many language schools. See dialogo-brazilstudy.com, www.transitionsabroad.com and www. applelanguages.com for more information.

## Money

### Currency

*£1 = R$5.27; €1 = R$4.36; US$1 = R$4 (Mar 2016).* The unit of currency is the **real**, R$ (plural **reais**). Any amount of foreign currency and 'a reasonable sum' in reais can be taken in, but sums over US$10,000 must be declared. Residents may only take out the equivalent of US$4000. Notes in circulation are: 100, 50, 10, 5 and 1 real; coins: 1 real, 50, 25, 10, 5 and 1 centavo. **Note** The exchange rate fluctuates – check regularly.

### Costs of travelling

Brazil is cheaper than most countries in South America though prices vary greatly. Rural areas can be 50% cheaper than heavily visited tourist areas in the big city. As a very rough guide, prices are about half those of Western Europe and a third cheaper than rural USA.

Hostel beds are usually around US$8. Budget hotels with few frills have rooms for as little as US$15, and you should have no difficulty finding a double room costing US$30 wherever you are. Rooms are often pretty much the same price whether 1 or 2 people are staying and aside from hostels prices invariably include a large breakfast.

Eating is generally inexpensive, especially in *padarias* (bakeries) or *comida por kilo* (pay by weight) restaurants, which offer a wide range of food (salads, meat, pasta and vegetarian). Expect to pay around US$4 to eat your fill in a good-value restaurant. Although bus travel is cheap by US or European standards, because of the long distances, costs can soon mount up. Internal flights prices have come down dramatically in the last couple of years and some routes work out cheaper than taking a bus, especially if booking online.

## ATMs

ATMs, or cash machines, are easy to come by. As well as being the most convenient way of withdrawing money, they frequently offer the best available rates of exchange. They are usually closed after 2130. There are 2 international ATM acceptance systems, **Plus** and **Cirrus**. Many issuers of debit and credit cards are linked to one, or both (eg Visa is Plus, MasterCard is Cirrus). **Bradesco** and **HSBC** are the 2 main banks offering this service. **Red Banco 24 Horas** kiosks advertise that they take a long list of credit cards in their ATMs, including MasterCard and Amex, but international cards cannot always be used; the same is true of **Banco do Brasil**.

Advise your bank before leaving, as cards are usually stopped in Brazil without prior warning. Find out before you leave what international functionality your card has. Check if your bank or credit card company imposes handling charges. Internet banking is useful for monitoring your account or transferring funds. Do not rely on one card, in case of loss. If you do lose a card, immediately contact the 24-hr helpline of the issuer in your home country (keep this number in a safe place).

## Exchange

Banks in major cities will change cash and, for those who still use them, traveller's cheques (TCs). If you keep the official exchange slips, you may convert back into foreign currency up to 50% of the amount you exchanged. The parallel market, found in travel agencies, exchange houses and among hotel staff, often offers marginally better rates than the banks but commissions can be very high. Many banks may only change US$300 minimum in cash, US$500 in TCs. Rates for TCs are usually far lower than for cash, they are harder to change and a very heavy commission may be charged.

## Credit cards

Credit cards are widely used. Visa and Mastercard are the most widely used, with **Diners Club** and **Amex** a close second. Cash advances on credit cards will only be paid in reais at the tourist rate, incurring at least a 1.5% commission. Banks in remote places may refuse to give a cash advance: try asking for the *gerente* (manager).

## Currency cards

If you don't want to carry lots of cash, prepaid currency cards allow you to preload money from your bank account, fixed at the day's exchange rate. They look like a credit or debit card and are issued by specialist money changing companies, such as **Travelex** and **Caxton FX**, as well as the **Post Office**. You can top up and check your balance by phone, online and sometimes by text.

## Money transfers

Money sent to Brazil is normally paid out in Brazilian currency, so do not have more sent out than you need for your stay. Funds can ostensibly be received within 48 banking hours, but it can take at least a month to arrive, allowing banks to capitalize on your transfer. The documentation required to receive it varies according to the whim of the bank staff, making the whole procedure often far more trouble than it is worth.

## Opening hours

Generally Mon-Fri 0900-1800; closed for lunch sometime between 1130 and 1400. **Shops** Also open on Sat until 1230 or 1300. **Government offices** Mon-Fri 1100-1800. **Banks** Mon-Fri 1000-1600 or 1630; closed at weekends.

## Post

To send a standard letter or postcard to the USA costs US$0.65, to Europe US$0.90, to Australia or South Africa US0.65. Air mail should take about 7 days to or from Britain or the USA. Franked and registered (insured) letters are normally secure, but check that the amount franked is what you have paid, or the item will not arrive. Aerogrammes are most reliable. To avoid queues and obtain higher denomination stamps go to the stamp desk at the main post office.

The post office sells cardboard boxes for sending packages internally and abroad. Rates and rules for sending literally vary from post office to post office even within the same town and the quickest service is **SEDEX**. The most widespread courier service is **Federal Express**, www.fedex.com/br. They are often cheaper than parcel post.

Postes restantes usually only hold letters for 30 days. Identification is required and it's a good idea to write your name on a piece of paper to help the attendant find your letters. Charges are minimal but often involve queuing at another counter to buy stamps, which are attached to your letter and franked before it is given to you.

## Safety See also page 27.

Mugging can take place anywhere. Travel light after dark with few valuables (avoid wearing jewellery and use a cheap, plastic, digital watch). Ask hotel staff where is and isn't safe; crime is patchy in Bahia. While Salvador and some of the cities of the Bahian interior can be unsafe anywhere after dark (and you are advised to take a cab), places like Caraíva, Trancoso and Itacaré see little crime at all.

If the worst does happen and you are threatened, don't panic, and hand over your valuables. Do not resist, and report the crime to the local tourist police later. It is extremely rare for a tourist to be hurt during a robbery in Brazil. Being aware of the dangers, acting confidently and using your common sense will reduce many of the risks.

Photocopy your passport, air ticket and other documents, make a record of traveller's cheque and credit card numbers. Keep them separately from the originals and leave another set of records at home. Keep all documents secure; hide your main cash supply in different places or under your clothes. Extra pockets sewn inside shirts and trousers, money belts (best worn below the waist), neck or leg pouches and elasticated support bandages for keeping money above the elbow or below the knee have been repeatedly recommended.

Violence over land ownership in parts of the interior have resulted in a 'Wild West' atmosphere in some towns, which should therefore be passed through quickly. Red-light districts should also be given a wide berth as there are reports of drinks being drugged with a substance popularly known as 'good night Cinderella'. This leaves the victim easily amenable to having their possessions stolen, or worse.

## Avoiding cons

Never trust anyone telling sob stories or offering 'safe rooms', and when looking for a hotel, always choose the room yourself. Be wary of 'plain-clothes policemen'; insist on seeing identification and on going to the police station by main roads. Do not hand over your identification (or money) until you are at the station. On no account take them directly back to your hotel. Be even more suspicious if they seek confirmation of their status from a passer-by.

## Hotel security

Hotel safe deposits are generally, but not always, secure. If you cannot get a receipt for valuables in a hotel safe, you can seal the contents in a plastic bag and sign across the seal. Always keep an inventory of what you have deposited. If you don't trust the hotel, lock everything in your pack and secure it in your room when you go out. If you lose valuables, report to the police and note details of the report for insurance purposes. Be sure to be present whenever your credit card is used.

## Police

There are several types of police: **Polícia Federal**, civilian dressed, who handle all federal law duties, including immigration. A subdivision is the **Polícia Federal Rodoviária**, uniformed, who are the traffic police on federal highways. **Polícia Militar** are the uniformed, street police force, under the control of the state governor, handling all state laws. They are not the same as the Armed Forces' internal police. **Polícia Civil**, also state controlled, handle local laws and investigations. They are usually in civilian dress, unless in the traffic division. In cities, the *prefeitura* controls the **Guarda Municipal**, who handles security. **Tourist police** operate in places with a strong tourist presence. In case of difficulty, visitors should seek out tourist police in the first instance.

## Public transport

When you have all your luggage with you at a bus or railway station, be especially careful and carry any shoulder bags in front of you. To be extra safe, take a taxi between the airport/bus station/railway station and hotel, keep your bags with you and pay only when you and your luggage are outside; avoid night buses and arriving at your destination at night.

## Sexual assault

If you are the victim of a sexual assault, you are advised firstly to contact a doctor (this can be your home doctor). You will need tests to determine whether you have contracted any STDs; you may also need advice on emergency contraception. You should contact your embassy, where consular staff will be very willing to help.

## Women travellers

Most of these tips apply to any single traveller. When you set out, err on the side of caution until your instincts have adjusted to the customs of a new culture. Be prepared for the exceptional curiosity extended to visitors, especially women, and try not to overreact. If, as a single woman, you can befriend a local woman, you will learn much more about the country you are visiting. There is a definite 'gringo trail' you can follow, which can be helpful when looking for safe accommodation, especially if arriving after dark (best avoided). Remember that for a single woman a taxi at night can be as dangerous as walking alone. It is easier for men to take the friendliness of locals at face value; women may be subject to unwanted attention. Do not disclose to strangers where you are staying. By wearing a wedding ring and saying that your 'husband' is close at hand, you may dissuade an aspiring suitor. If politeness fails, do not feel bad about showing offence and departing. A good rule is always to act with confidence, as though you know where you are going, even if you do not. Someone who looks lost is more likely to attract unwanted attention.

## Student travellers

If you are in full-time education you will be entitled to an **ISIC** (International Student Identity Card), which is valid in more than 77 countries. The ISIC card gives you special prices on transport and access to a variety of other concessions and services. For the location of your nearest ISIC office see www.isic.org. ISIC cards can be obtained in Brazil from **STB** agencies throughout the country; also try www.carteiradoestudante.com.br, which is in Portuguese but easy to follow (click 'pontos de Venda' for details of agencies). Remember to take photographs when having a card issued.

In practice, the ISIC card is rarely recognized or accepted for discounts outside of the south and southeast of Brazil, but is nonetheless useful for obtaining half-price entry to the cinema. Youth hostels will often accept it in lieu of a **HI** card or at least give a discount, and some university accommodation (and subsidized canteens) will allow very cheap short-term stays to holders.

## Tax

**Airport departure tax** The amount of tax depends on the class and size of the airport, but the cost is usually incorporated into the ticket.

**VAT** Rates vary from 7-25% at state and federal level; the average is 17-20%. The tax is generally included in the international or domestic ticket price.

## Telephone *Country code: +55.*

Ringing: equal tones with long pauses. Engaged: equal tones, equal pauses.

Making a phone call in Brazil can be confusing. It is necessary to dial a 2-digit telephone company code prior to the area code for all calls. Phone numbers are now printed in this way: 0XX21 (0 for a national call, XX for the code of the phone company chosen (eg 31 for Telemar) followed by, 21 for Rio de Janeiro, for example, and the 8 or 9-digit number of the subscriber. The same is true for international calls where 00 is followed by the operator code and then the country code and number.

Telephone operators and their codes are: **Embratel**, 21 (nationwide); **Telefônica**, 15 (state of São Paulo); **Telemar**, 31 (Alagoas, Amazonas, Amapá, Bahia, Ceará, Espírito Santo, Maranhão, most of Minas Gerais, Pará, Paraíba, Pernambuco, Piauí, Rio de Janeiro, Rio Grande do Norte, Roraima, Sergipe); **Tele Centro-Sul**, 14 (Acre, Goiás, Mato Grosso, Mato Grosso do Sul, Paraná, Rondônia, Santa Catarina, Tocantins and the cities of Brasília and Pelotas); **CTBC-Telecom**, 12 (some parts of Minas Gerais, Goiás, Mato Grosso do Sul and São Paulo state); **Intelig**, 23.

### National calls

Telephone booths or *orelhões* (literally 'big ears' as they are usually ear-shaped, fibreglass shells) are easy to come by in towns and cities. Local phone calls and telegrams are cheap.

*Cartões telefônicos* (phone cards) are available from newsstands, post offices and some chemists. They cost US$3 for 30 units and up to US$5 for 90 units. Local calls from a private phone are often free. *Cartões telefônicos internacionais* (international phone cards) are increasingly available in tourist areas and are often sold at hostels.

### Mobile phones and apps

Cellular phones are widespread and coverage excellent even in remote areas, but prices are extraordinarily high and users still pay to receive calls outside the metropolitan area where their phone is registered. SIM cards are hard to buy as users require a CPF (a Brazilian social security number) to buy one, but phones can be hired. When using a cellular telephone you do not drop the zero from the area code as you have to when dialling from a fixed line.

Some networks, eg **O2**, provide an app so you can use the time on your contract in your home country if you access the app via Wi-Fi. Internet calls (eg via **Skype**, **Whatsapp** and **Viber**) are also possible if you have access to Wi-Fi.

There are many Brazilian travel guide apps available only a fraction of which are thoroughly researched. Fewer still are updated regularly. You are far better off using Google Maps and asking in the hotel or from local people.

## Time

Brazil has 4 time zones: Brazilian standard time is GMT-3; the Amazon time zone (Pará west of the Rio Xingu, Amazonas, Roraima, Rondônia, Mato Grosso and Mato Grosso do Sul) is GMT-4, the State of Acre is GMT-5; and the Fernando de Noronha archipelago is GMT-2. Clocks move forward 1 hr in summer for approximately 5 months (usually between Oct and Feb or Mar), but times of change vary. This does not apply to Acre.

## Tipping

Tipping is not usual, but always appreciated as staff are often paid a pittance. In restaurants, add 10% of the bill if no service charge is included; cloakroom attendants deserve a small tip; porters have fixed charges but often receive tips as well; unofficial car parkers on city streets should be tipped R$2.

## Tourist information

The **Ministério do Turismo**, www.braziltour. com, is in charge of tourism in Brazil. Local tourist information bureaux are not usually helpful for information on cheap hotels, they generally just dish out pamphlets. Expensive hotels provide tourist magazines for their guests. Telephone directories (not Rio) contain good street maps.

Other good sources of information are: **LATA**, www.lata.org. The Latin American Travel Association, with useful country information and listings of all UK operators specializing in Latin America. Also has up-to-date information on public safety, health, weather, travel costs, economics and politics highlighted for each nation. Wide selection of Latin American maps available, as well as individual travel planning assistance.
**South American Explorers**, T607-277 0488, www.saexplorers.org. A non-profit educational organization functioning primarily as an information network for South America. Useful for travellers to Brazil and the rest of the continent.

### National parks

National parks are run by the Brazilian institute of environmental protection, **Ibama**, T061-3316 1212, www.ibama.gov.br (in Portuguese only). For information, contact **Linha Verde**, T0800-618080, linhaverde.sede@ibama. gov.br. National parks are open to visitors, usually with a permit from Ibama. See also the **Ministério do Meio Ambiente** website, www.mma.gov.br (in Portuguese only).

## Useful websites

**www.brazil.org.uk** Provides a broad range of info on Brazilian history and culture from the UK Brazilian embassy.
**www.brazilmax.com** Excellent information on culture and lifestyle, the best available in English.
**www.visitbrazil.com** The official tourism website of Brazil, and the best.
**www.gringos.com.br** An excellent source of information on all things Brazilian for visitors and expats.
**www.ipanema.com** A quirky, informative site on all things Rio de Janeiro.
**www.maria-brazil.org** A wonderfully personal introduction to Brazil, specifically Rio, featuring Maria's cookbook and little black book, features and reviews.
**www.socioambiental.org** Invaluable for up-to-the-minute, accurate information on environmental and indigenous issues. In Portuguese only.
**www.survival-international.org** The world's leading campaign organization for indigenous peoples with excellent information on various Brazilian indigenous groups.
**www.worldtwitch.com** Birding information and comprehensive listings of rainforest lodges.

## Tour operators

**UK**
### Brazil specialists
**Bespoke Brazil**, T01603-340680, www.bespokebrazil.com. Tailor-made trips throughout the country, even to the lesser-known areas.
**Brazil Revealed**, T01932-424252, www.brazilrevealed.co.uk. A specialist, boutique and bespoke operator with excellent in-country contacts.
**Hidden Pousadas Brazil**, www.hidden pousadasbrazil.com. A choice of tasteful small hotels and homestays hand-picked from all over the country and ranging from chic but simple to luxe and languorous.

**Journey Latin America**, T020-8600 1881, www.journeylatinamerica.co.uk. An enormous range of Brazil trips, including bespoke options.

**SJ Villas**, T020-7351 6384, www.sjvillas.co.uk. Luxurious houses on the Bahian beaches.

**Sunvil Latin America**, T020-8758 4774, www.sunvil.co.uk. Quality packages and tailor-made trips throughout the country.

**Veloso Tours**, T020-8762 0616, www.veloso.com. Imaginative tours throughout Brazil; bespoke options on request.

### Wildlife and birding specialists
**Naturetrek**, T01962-733051, www.naturetrek.co.uk. Wildlife tours throughout Brazil with bespoke options and specialist birding tours of the Atlantic coastal rainforests.

**Ornitholidays**, T01794-519445, www.ornitholidays.co.uk. Annual or biannual birding trips throughout Brazil, including the Atlantic coast rainforest.

**Reef and Rainforest Tours Ltd**, T01803-866965, www.reefandrainforest.co.uk. Specialists in tailor-made and group wildlife tours.

### North America
**Brazil For Less**, T1-877-565 8119 (US toll free) or T+44-203-006 2507 (UK), www.brazilforless.com. US-based travel firm with a focus solely on South America, with local offices and operations, and a price guarantee. Good-value tours, run by travellers for travellers. Will meet or beat any internet rates from outside Brazil.

### Wildlife and birding specialists
**Field Guides**, T1-800-7284953, www.fieldguides.com. Interesting birdwatching tours to all parts of Brazil.

**Focus Tours**, T(505)216 7780, www.focustours.com. Environmentally responsible travel throughout Brazil.

### Brazil
**Dehouche**, T021-2512 3895, www.dehouche.com. Upmarket, carefully tailored trips throughout Brazil.

**Matueté**, T011-3071 4515, www.matuete.com. Bespoke luxury options around Brazil with a range of private house rentals.

**Tatur Turismo**, T071-3114 7900, www.tatur.com.br. Very helpful and professional bespoke Bahia-based agency who can organize tours throughout Bahia, using smaller hotels.

**whl.travel**, T031-3889 8596, www.whl.travel. Online network of tour operators for booking accommodation and tours throughout Brazil.

### Wildlife and birding specialists
**Andy and Nadime Whittaker's Birding Brazil Tours**, www.birdingbraziltours.com. A good company, based in Manaus. The couple worked with the BBC Natural History Unit on David Attenborough's *The Life of Birds* and are ground agents for a number of the

Visit Brazil with the specialists

**bespoke brazil**
TAILOR-MADE HOLIDAYS TO BRAZIL

www.bespokebrazil.com
Tel: +44 (0) 1603 340680

major birding tour companies from the US and Europe.

**Birding Brazil Tours**, www.birdingbrazil tours.com. First-class bespoke options throughout the country.

**Edson Endrigo**, www.avesfoto.com.br. Bespoke options only.

## Visas and immigration

Visas are not required for stays of up to 90 days by tourists from Andorra, Argentina, Austria, Bahamas, Barbados, Belgium, Bolivia, Chile, Colombia, Costa Rica, Denmark, Ecuador, Finland, France, Germany, Greece, Iceland, Ireland, Italy, Liechtenstein, Luxembourg, Malaysia, Monaco, Morocco, Namibia, the Netherlands, Norway, Paraguay, Peru, Philippines, Portugal, San Marino, South Africa, Spain, Suriname, Sweden, Switzerland, Thailand, Trinidad and Tobago, United Kingdom, Uruguay, the Vatican and Venezuela. For them, only the following documents are required at the port of disembarkation: a passport valid for at least 6 months (or *cédula de identidad* for nationals of Argentina, Chile, Paraguay and Uruguay); and a return or onward ticket, or adequate proof that you can purchase your return fare, subject to no remuneration being received in Brazil and no legally binding or contractual documents being signed. Venezuelan passport holders can stay for 60 days on filling in a form at the border.

Citizens of the USA, Canada, Australia, New Zealand and other countries not mentioned above, and anyone wanting to stay longer than 180 days, *must* get a visa before arrival, which may, if you ask, be granted for multiple entry. US citizens must be fingerprinted on entry to Brazil. Visa fees vary from country to country, so apply to the Brazilian consulate in your home country. The consular fee in the USA is US$50. Students planning to study in Brazil or employees of foreign companies can apply for a 1- or 2-year visa. 2 copies of the application form, 2 photos, a letter from the sponsoring company or educational institution in Brazil, a police form showing no criminal convictions and a fee of around US$70 is required.

### Extensions

Foreign tourists may stay a maximum of 180 days in any 1 year. 90-day renewals are easily obtainable, but only at least 15 days before the expiry of your 90-day permit, from the Polícia Federal. The procedure varies, but generally you have to: fill out 3 copies of the tax form at the Polícia Federal, take them to a branch of **Banco do Brasil,** pay US$15 and bring 2 copies back. You will then be given the extension form to fill in and be asked for your passport to stamp in the extension. According to regulations (which should be on display) you need to show a return ticket, cash, cheques or a credit card, a personal reference and proof of an address of a person living in the same city as the office (in practice you simply write this in the space on the form). Some offices will only give you an extension within 10 days of the expiry of your permit.

Some points of entry, such as the Colombian border, refuse entry for longer than 30 days, renewals are then for the same period, insist if you want 90 days. For longer stays you must leave the country and return (not the same day) to get a new 90-day permit. If your visa has expired, getting a new visa can be costly (US$35 for a consultation, US$30 for the visa itself) and may take anything up to 45 days, depending on where you apply. If you overstay your visa, or extension, you will be fined US$7 per day, with no upper limit. After paying the fine to Polícia Federal, you will be issued with an exit visa and must leave within 8 days.

Officially, if you leave Brazil within the 90-day permission to stay and then re-enter the country, you should only be allowed to stay until the 90-day permit expires. If, however, you are given another 90-day permit, this may lead to charges of overstaying if you apply for an extension.

## Identification

You must always carry identification when in Brazil. Take a photocopy of the personal details in your passport, plus your Brazilian immigration stamp, and leave your passport in the hotel safe deposit. This photocopy, when authorized in a *cartório*, US$1, is a legitimate copy of your documents. Be prepared, however, to present the originals when travelling in sensitive border areas. Always keep an independent record of your passport details. Also register with your consulate to expedite document replacement if yours gets lost or stolen.

**Warning** Do not lose the entry/exit permit they give you when you enter Brazil. Leaving the country without it, you may have to pay up to US$100 per person. It is suggested that you photocopy this form and have it authenticated at a *cartório*, US$1, in case of loss or theft.

## Weights and measures

Metric.

# Footnotes

# **Basic** Portuguese for travellers

Learning Portuguese is a useful part of the preparation for a trip to Brazil and no volume of dictionaries, phrase books or word lists will provide the same enjoyment as being able to communicate directly with the people of the country you are visiting. It is a good idea to make an effort to grasp the basics before you go. As you travel you will pick up more of the language and the more you know, the more you will benefit from your stay.

## General pronunciation

Within Brazil itself, there are variations in pronunciation, intonation, phraseology and slang. This makes for great richness and for the possibility of great enjoyment in the language. A couple of points which the newcomer to the language will spot immediately are the use of the tilde (~) over 'a' and 'o'. This makes the vowel nasal, as does a word ending in 'm' or 'ns', or a vowel followed by 'm' + consonant, or by 'n' + consonant. Another important point of spelling is that for words ending in 'i' and 'u' the emphasis is on the last syllable, though (unlike Spanish) no accent is used. This is especially relevant in place names like Buriti, Guarapari, Caxambu, Iguaçu. Note also the use of 'ç', which changes the pronunciation of c from hard [k] to soft [s].

## Personal pronouns

In conversation, most people refer to 'you' as *você*, although in the south and in Pará *tu* is more common. To be more polite, use *O Senhor/A Senhora*. For 'us', *gente* (people, folks) is very common when it includes you too.

## Portuguese words and phrases

### Greetings and courtesies

| | |
|---|---|
| hello | *oi/olá* |
| good morning | *bom dia* |
| good afternoon | *boa tarde* |
| good evening/night | *boa noite* |
| goodbye | *adeus/tchau* |
| see you later | *até logo* |
| please | *por favor/faz favor* |
| thank you | *obrigado* (if a man is speaking)/ *obrigada* (if a woman is speaking) |
| thank you very much | *muito obrigado/muito obrigada* |
| how are you? | *como vai você tudo bem?/tudo bom?* |
| I am fine | *vou bem/tudo bem* |
| pleased to meet you | *um prazer* |
| no | *não* |
| yes | *sim* |
| excuse me | *com licença* |
| I don't understand | *não entendo* |
| please speak slowly | *fale devagar por favor* |
| what is your name? | *qual é seu nome?* |
| my name is… | *o meu nome é…* |
| go away! | *vai embora!* |

## Basic questions

| | |
|---|---|
| where is? | *onde está/onde fica?* |
| why? | *por que?* |
| how much does it cost? | *quanto custa?* |
| what for? | *para que?* |
| how much is it? | *quanto é?* |
| how do I get to…? | *para chegar a…?* |
| when? | *quando?* |
| I want to go to… | *quero ir para…* |
| when does the bus leave?/arrive? | *a que hor sai/chega o ônibus?* |
| is this the way to the church? | *aquí é o caminho para a igreja?* |

## Basics

| | |
|---|---|
| bathroom/toilet | *banheiro* |
| police (policeman) | *a polícia (o polícia)* |
| hotel | *o (a pensão, a hospedaria)* |
| restaurant | *o restaurante (o lanchonete)* |
| post office | *o correio* |
| telephone office (central) | *telefônica* |
| supermarket | *o supermercado* |
| market | *o mercado* |
| bank | *o banco* |
| bureau de change | *a casa de câmbio* |
| exchange rate | *a taxa de câmbio* |
| notes/coins | *notas/moedas* |
| traveller's cheques | *os travelers/os cheques de viagem* |
| cash | *dinheiro* |
| breakfast | *o caféde manh* |
| lunch | *o almoço* |
| dinner/supper | *o jantar* |
| Meal | *a refeição* |
| drink | *a bebida* |
| mineral water | *a água mineral* |
| soft fizzy drink | *o refrigerante* |
| beer | *a cerveja* |
| without sugar | *sem açúcar* |
| without meat | *sem carne* |

## Getting around

| | |
|---|---|
| on the left/right | *à esquerda/à direita* |
| straight on | *direto* |
| to walk | *caminhar* |
| bus station | *a rodoviária* |
| bus | *o ônibus* |
| bus stop | *a parada* |
| train | *a trem* |
| airport | *o aeroporto* |
| aeroplane/airplane | *o avião* |

| | |
|---|---|
| flight | *o vôa* |
| first/second class | *primeira/segunda clase* |
| train station | *a ferroviária* |
| combined bus and train station | *a rodoferroviária* |
| ticket | *o passagem/o bilhete* |
| ticket office | *a bilheteria* |

## Accommodation

| | |
|---|---|
| room | *quarto* |
| noisy | *barulhento* |
| single/double room | *(quarto de) solteiro/(quarto para) casal* |
| room with two beds | *quarto com duas camas* |
| with private bathroom | *quarto com banheiro* |
| hot/cold water | *água quente/fria* |
| to make up/clean | *limpar* |
| sheet(s) | *o lençol (os lençóis)* |
| blankets | *as mantas* |
| pillow | *o travesseiro* |
| clean/dirty towels | *as toalhas limpas/sujas* |
| toilet paper | *o papel higiêico* |

## Health

| | |
|---|---|
| chemist | *a farmacia* |
| doctor | *o coutor/a doutora* |
| (for) pain | *(para) dor* |
| stomach | *o esômago (a barriga)* |
| head | *a cabeça* |
| fever/sweat | *a febre/o suor higiênicas* |
| diarrhoea | *a diarréia* |
| blood | *o sangue* |
| condoms | *as camisinhas/os preservativos* |
| contraceptive (pill) | *anticonceptional (a pílula)* |
| period | *a menstruação/a regra* |
| sanitary towels/tampons | *toalhas absorventes/absorventes internos* |
| contact lenses | *lentes de contacto* |
| aspirin | *a aspirina* |

## Time

| | |
|---|---|
| at one o'clock (am/pm) | *a uma hota (da manhã/da tarde)* |
| at half past two/two thirty | *as dois e meia* |
| at a quarter to three | *quinze para as três* |
| it's one o'clock | *é uma* |
| it's seven o'clock | *são sete horas* |
| it's twenty past six/six twenty | *são seis e vinte* |
| it's five to nine | *são cinco para as nove* |
| in ten minutes | *em dez minutos* |
| five hours | *cinco horas* |
| does it take long? | *sura muito?* |

## Days

| | | | |
|---|---|---|---|
| Monday | *segunda feiro* | Friday | *sexta feira* |
| Tuesday | *terça feira* | Saturday | *sábado* |
| Wednesday | *quarta feira* | Sunday | *domingo* |
| Thursday | *quinta feira* | | |

## Months

| | | | |
|---|---|---|---|
| January | *janeiro* | July | *julho* |
| February | *fevereiro* | August | *agosto* |
| March | *março* | September | *setembro* |
| April | *abril* | October | *outubro* |
| May | *maio* | November | *novembro* |
| June | *junho* | December | *dezembro* |

## Numbers

| | | | |
|---|---|---|---|
| one | *um/uma* | fifteen | *quinze* |
| two | *dois/duas* | sixteen | *dezesseis* |
| three | *três* | seventeen | *dezessete* |
| four | *quatro* | eighteen | *dezoito* |
| five | *cinco* | nineteen | dezenove |
| six | *seis* ('*meia*' half, is frequently used for number 6 ie half-dozen) | twenty | *vinte* |
| | | twenty-one | *vente e um* |
| | | thirty | *trinta* |
| | | forty | *cuarenta* |
| seven | *sete* | fifty | *cinqüe* |
| eight | *oito* | sixty | *sessenta* |
| nine | *nove* | seventy | *setenta* |
| ten | *dez* | eighty | *oitenta* |
| eleven | *onze* | ninety | *noventa* |
| twelve | *doze* | hundred | *cem, cento* |
| thirteen | *treze* | thousand | *mil* |
| fourteen | *catorze* | | |

## Useful slang

| | |
|---|---|
| that's great/cool | *que legal* |
| bloke/guy/geezer | *cara* (literally 'face'), *mano* |
| cheesy/tacky | *brega* |
| in fashion/cool | *descolado* |